BEYOND FAILURE

Discovering Grace and Hope in the Hard Times of Life

James A. Scudder

CROSSWAY BOOKS • WHEATON, ILLINOIS
A DIVISION OF GOOD NEWS PUBLISHERS

Beyond Failure

Published by Crossway Books
a division of Good News Publishers
1300 Crescent Street
Wheaton, Illinois 60187

Cover design: Liita Forsyth

Cover illustration: PhotoDisc™/Gary Irving

First printing 2001

Printed in the United States of America

Scripture is taken from the King James Version of the Bible.

Library of Congress Cataloging-in-Publication Data

Scudder, James A., 1946-
Beyond failure: discovering grace and hope in the hard times of life / James A. Scudder.
p. cm.
ISBN 1-58134-250-0 (pbk. : alk. paper)
1. Success—Religious aspects—Christianity. 2. Failure (Christian theology) 3. Success—Biblical teaching. 4. Failure (Christian theology)—Biblical teaching. 5. Peter, the Apostle, Saint. I. Title.
BV4598.3 .S43 2001
248.8'6—dc21 00-010843
CIP

15 14 13 12 11 10 09 08 07 06 05 04 03 02 01
15 14 13 12 11 10 9 8 7 6 5 4 3 2 1

Contents

Foreword

I am delighted to share my appreciation for a book that I believe every believer should read. We are living in the most challenging days ever. We have money and buildings, and we have top-notch educational institutions to prepare our leaders. We have an abundance of books, tapes, conferences, training centers, and parachurch ministries, but inauthentic Christian living negates all of these advantages.

A young boy who had much ambition and desire to succeed asked his mentor the question: "How can I make a name for myself in life?"

His mentor replied, "To get the attention of people, you have to be successful."

The boy then asked, "How can I be successful?"

His mentor said, "By getting the experience."

"How do I get experience?"

The answer: "By making right decisions."

"How do I make right decisions?"

"By learning what happens to you when you make wrong decisions."

Of course, the only way we as Christians can make right decisions is to obey the Spirit of God, who was given to us by God to enable us to make those right decisions. However, we know that the life of every victorious Christian is determined by how well that person handles failure. We know that not all apparent failures are direct attacks from Satan. One of the delights of God is to see how His children trust Him and thank Him when everything appears to go wrong. Ephesians 3:13 says, "Wherefore I desire that ye faint not at my tribulation for you, which is your glory." First

Thessalonians 5:18 reminds us to give thanks in everything, for this is the will of God in Christ Jesus concerning us.

As Job was God's delightful exhibit before Satan, so also are we His display as we handle the failures God permits to come our way. We know that Satan's most effective weapon against every Christian is DISCOURAGEMENT. Discouraged Christians are defeated Christians, and a defeated Christian spreads discouragement to others. Defeated Christians are not soul-winners. It has often been said, "You can tell how steadfast a Christian is by how much it takes for him to get discouraged."

For many years I have known James Scudder, the author of this excellent book. I consider him a special friend and an inspiration. During this time I have seen him go through many challenging years with the construction of the two Quentin Road Baptist Churches. You will read in this book much about the discouragement that came from this construction alone. This book is truly a living testimony of a man that God has blessed abundantly because he learned through many failures that the setback was God's way of spelling victory if God received the glory.

I believe that one of the main reasons God has blessed the ministry at Quentin Road has been because James Scudder has always majored on preaching the beautiful, clear, life-giving message of God's grace that was finished at Calvary. It is one thing to believe that message, as many do, but it is another thing to make proclaiming it to a lost and dying world the entire focus of your life. Yes, I urge you to read this book, for I believe it will greatly encourage you in your walk with the Lord.

ART ROHRHEIM
President Emeritus/Founder
Awana Clubs International

1

EVEN THE BEST FAIL

OPTIMISTIC AND NEWLY GRADUATED from Bible college, I felt I could conquer the world for Jesus Christ. After all, how hard could it be to start a church? I guessed I was thinking conservatively when I estimated that after my first month as a preacher, I probably would have 100 members. And after a year I thought maybe my church would have 1,000 people.

But those early days were hard. I could never have been totally prepared for how difficult that time would be. I had to work two jobs to earn enough money to pay our bills. My dear wife, Linda, had to work. Even with both of us employed, all we could afford was a small apartment in a bad part of the city. We didn't have curtains or much furniture. Our two children were still in diapers, and Linda and I hardly saw each other as we struggled to raise them, work our jobs, and start a church. After a few months I began to realize just how difficult this undertaking really was.

And if that weren't enough, people were asking why I had come to Chicago when there were already so many well-established ministries in the area. I only knew that God had called me, and that's why I had moved. But all these pressures began to undermine my confidence, and I was beginning to question myself.

We found a small storefront for the church to meet in—a very small storefront. Faithfully Linda and I met there week after week, praying and hoping people would come. I witnessed to people in the neighborhood whenever I could, and though many came to know the Lord, I began to find out that it was a challenge to get them to come to church.

Sometimes a few people trickled through the doors, and we would have a small group. We would get so excited, only to be disappointed because in a few weeks they would stop coming. We came to realize that the gangs in the area kept people from attending regularly.

I cried out to the Lord, "Why don't we have more people? What am I doing wrong? Linda and I are tired, Lord. We are both working full-time jobs to make ends meet, and we're trying to start this church and get it going. Yet it seems like nothing is happening! You know we're struggling to put food on the table for our children. I hate to see Linda struggle so much. What do we need to do to make this church grow? No matter what I try, nothing works. Where is Your presence, Lord? I thought You would be here with me, helping me to do Your work."

At first it seemed as if God hadn't heard my prayers. In my moments of hopelessness, I felt that the Lord had abandoned me. I was terribly discouraged and felt like a failure.

One day a young man named Paul, whom I had led to the Lord some time before, gave me a gift. When I opened the package, I found a small replica of a Civil War cannon. Inside the barrel of the cannon was a rolled-up note. I fished it out and read these words: "Pastor Scudder, I know you are discouraged. But hang in there. I have no doubt that someday you will have a vibrant, growing ministry here in Chicago."

For me new meaning came to the verse that tells us not to be weary in well doing, for in due season, we will see the reward (Galatians 6:9). Through Paul's encouragement, God had given me tangible evidence that He was still with me. I felt renewed courage to continue with the work God had called me to do.

Slowly but surely we began to see real and lasting results. God was faithful and gave us help when we least expected it. I've now been a pastor for more than twenty-eight years, and over that time I have seen God's hand work in many surprising ways. Eventually I came to realize that He doesn't always work in the way I want Him to. His ways are much greater than anything I could imagine. I discovered that all we could do was keep serving and place our frustrations and worries in God's hands. Now, many years later, we have many people in our congregation. God has blessed our many years of hard work. But I have never forgotten those difficult early days; they helped to shape and train us.

God's Faithfulness in Our Failures

Throughout my years in ministry, there have been a number of times when I felt like a failure. Yet God never once failed me. I know I could easily have become like a pastor I heard about, who finally decided he couldn't take it anymore. A few onlookers became momentarily curious when they saw him drive into the church parking lot in a borrowed pickup truck. But the pastor really got their attention when he backed the truck across the lawn to his study door. Refusing assistance, he began to empty everything in his office onto the truck bed. First he dumped his desk drawers and his files. Last was his library of books, which he tossed carelessly into a heap. His task done, he left the church for good.

It was later learned that he drove to the city dump where he threw everything into the garbage pile. It was his way of putting behind him the overwhelming sense of failure and loss that he had experienced in his ministry. This young pastor was determined never to return to the ministry.[1]

That could have been me. Yet by the grace of God it wasn't. The encouragement I received along the way helped me. I also began to recognize God's hand working in my life in spite of the mistakes I made. I began to see that God was with me every step of the way. He wasn't so much interested in how many people I had in my church as He was concerned about whether I would be faithful to Him.

Many times I have wished I could go back to those early days and start over, knowing what I know now. However, this isn't God's way. He knew I was going to fail Him, but He also knew that I needed those experiences in order to learn that He would never fail me.

Is this true in your life? Do you feel like I did when I first started my ministry as a pastor? Do you feel as if everything has gone wrong and even the Lord has abandoned you? Dear friend, I would encourage you to take a moment to reflect on the faithfulness of God. He is with you right now and has never left you. He is the friend that will stay closer to you than even your own family (Proverbs 18:24). Take a moment now to thank God for His faithfulness toward you. Realize that the strength you need comes from a divine Source—and this Source never runs dry!

When You Don't Know You've Failed

To pay for his schooling, Bob worked at a septic tank cleaning company. At first the smells he encountered bothered him, but after a while he didn't notice them as much.

One day an emergency job called him out of class. He was working frantically to drain an overloaded septic tank when the line broke, spraying him with a light coating of sewage. He desperately needed to take a final test, so he went back to class without showering. As he neared the open doors of the elevator at school, he saw the girl of his dreams already inside. He had had his eye on her for some time and had been trying to get up the courage to ask her for a date.

Anxious to make a good impression, he stood a little taller and stepped in. The door closed. Nothing could have prepared Bob for what happened next. The girl took one whiff and promptly fainted. Bob quickly pushed the emergency button to open the doors and saw the girl's parents standing outside the elevator. Delicately holding her nose, the girl's mother gave him a long look as she hurried to help her recovering daughter. Bob was glad to disappear.

Everyone knew that Bob reeked of sewage that day except Bob. And sometimes it can be the same way in the Christian life. Everyone else seems to know the right lingo, the correct worship posture, and the proper prayer techniques, but somehow no one has ever told you their secret to living victoriously.

You want to be successful and serve the Lord. Yet you see yourself failing every day. Does it seem that other believers are so much further ahead that you could never catch up? Maybe after you hear an inspiring sermon, you think you've finally learned the secret, only to fail in some way the following week. Maybe you succumb to temptation, you say a careless word, or your devotional times with God taper off. Whatever the case, you feel you just don't measure up as a Christian. You're a failure. Perhaps you feel like a failure because you can't live up to other people's expectations. Maybe your mother and father put such high expectations on you that you never thought you could please them.

A young man I knew in college felt this way. As he was growing up, he was constantly compared to his older brother. His parents would say, "You aren't as good in math as your brother," or, "Your brother is better than you at track." These comments discouraged this man to the point that even though he was an overachiever himself and actually quite successful, he could never get over the stigma of not being exactly like his older brother.

It is important that we don't base our expectations of success on whether we are as good as someone else. Every one of us is a unique creation of God, and every one of us has a different purpose and calling in the Christian life. Radio teacher and writer Warren Wiersbe affirmed this when he said, "Keeping in mind that the Lord is the final judge of our service helps set us free from the fear of people and the desire to please them at the expense of pleasing God. We can't please everybody, nor should we try. Our aim should be to walk and to please God."[2] "As ye have received of us how ye ought to walk and to please God, so ye would abound more and more" (1 Thessalonians 4:1).

Wiersbe's observation is important: We should live only to please God, not people. It's God's standard of success that counts, not the world's. When we live to please God, we will immediately remove from our shoulders the unbearable weight of the world's expectations, and as a result, get rid of many of our feelings of failure at once.

The Fear of Failure

There are some people who *aren't* failures, and yet they *fear* failure. The fear of failure can cause sleepless nights and stressed-out days. It has driven good people to alcohol and drugs. It can result in depression that consumes and destroys. It can make employees care only for themselves as they "climb the corporate ladder." It can cause businesses to go bankrupt and families to shatter.

The word *failure* is even taboo in our society. People will say that you shouldn't even say or think anything negative. As one popular author writes, "If you are thinking thoughts of defeat, I urge you to rid yourself of such thoughts, for as you think defeat, you tend to get it. Adopt the 'I don't believe in defeat' attitude."[3] I'm not saying that we should walk around thinking we are going to be defeated, but success is not going to come because we force ourselves not to think about failure. It is more important that we measure our success by the appropriate standards.

Many times when we think we have failed, it is because we have forgotten the true biblical definition of success and failure. Don't fall for the philosophy that says, "If you think you could fail, then you are setting yourself up to fail." In the upcoming chapters, we will see examples from God's Word of people who thought they couldn't fail, and yet they failed miserably. And we will see examples of those who learned where their true strength came from, and then they went on to become incredible successes.

A Biblical Perspective on Failure

It is important to remember that the world's definition of success (a fine house, a perfect family, an expensive car, and a high salary) is very different from the biblical definition of success. Therefore the world's definition of failure (not having the perfect car, house, etc.) is going to be much different from the biblical definition of failure.

Failure and success take on a new meaning when viewed from God's perspective. When you look at life from a heavenly vantage point, it's going to affect your priorities, goals, and accomplishments. It helps to remember that this world is temporary, and only what is done for Christ matters (Romans 12:1-2; 1 Corinthians 6:20). Your heavenly Father loves you and has a good plan for your life. In the Bible He reveals His desires for all that you and I do. So true success is responding to and obeying God's will for your life. And true failure is failing to heed God's Word and the wisdom He has written down in the Bible for you.

Sometimes following God's call on your life may lead you into difficult circumstances that make you feel like a failure. A certain vehicle I owned comes to my mind as an example. One evening, during the time when I was still establishing the church, Linda and I were driving home to our small apartment. Startled by a loud sound, I realized that the tire had blown out. Since we were in a hurry to get home, the delay frustrated me. It took awhile to fix the tire, so we arrived home later than planned. We were surprised to learn that the apartment below ours had been burglarized during the time the tire was fixed. Through the delay we had been spared possible harm. I took a moment right then to praise God for His wonderful timing! Even though a flat tire might be considered "difficult circumstances," those same circumstances may have saved our lives.

The Bible is full of such examples—people who faithfully

served God in spite of their challenging situations. Noah preached for 120 years, and he had only seven followers, yet he was a great success in God's eyes. The apostle Paul preached according to God's calling; consequently, he was rejected, beaten, and cast into prison. But from God's perspective, Paul was a success.

A supreme example is our Lord Jesus Christ. He was born in a lowly manger and wrapped in swaddling clothes. He grew up in a poor family. During his ministry, He had no place to call His own. Though He was a King, He was not a wealthy landowner, and He did not accumulate material wealth. He faced constant rejection and ridicule. The Jewish religious leaders hated Him and tried to kill Him. He was betrayed, rejected, and crucified. At the cross His little group of disciples abandoned Him. That doesn't sound very successful, does it? Yet He was the greatest success ever known.

Remember that if you are doing what God wants you to do, you are not a failure. God doesn't measure failure or success by the amount of material things He has given you or the achievements you've attained in this life. Instead, He is interested in your heart. We know that man looks on the outward appearance, but God looks on the heart (1 Samuel 16:7).

One of the reasons the Bible can be so relevant to our daily lives is that it not only records the successes of people, but it also records their failures. How many books can you find that devote just as much space to people's failures as to their successes? What the Bible does actually goes against the grain of what we read and hear today. It is not popular to talk about failure.

A God of Second Chances

Even when we *do* fail as Christians, God still remains faithful to us. He loves us in spite of our faults. An obvious proof of that love is the fact that Christ came to save sinners. He didn't come to save "holy" people. He came to save those who were lost and without hope.

Don't be surprised when you fail. In our humanness, we will make mistakes. But sometimes after we've failed repeatedly, we begin to feel that there's no hope—that we may as well give up. Or if we do something terribly wrong, we may think that God couldn't possibly forgive us or want to have anything to do with us.

But our God is a God of second chances. And third chances. And fourth. And fifth. And more! He has promised to be with us always, and He is willing to help us when we stumble along life's path. He's a loving, caring Father, a Great Shepherd. He longs to help us, if only we would trust Him and rest in His never-changing love toward us.

A Failure God Could Use

Even the great men and women of God have experienced failure. Not only have they failed, but also one of them even went so far as to deny that he even knew the Lord. This man was not a brand-new Christian who didn't know any better; he was one of Jesus' closest disciples!

The disciple's name was Peter. When I read the Gospels, I love to read about Peter's great love for the Lord. He was zealous. He was one of the first disciples to declare that Jesus Christ was indeed the Son of God (Matthew 16:16). Peter's name appears frequently in connection with Jesus' ministry. He seems to play a prominent role in all that we read in the Gospels. One commentator mentions that there must have been something in his natural disposition and character that the Lord immediately recognized as offering the possibilities of a noble life and noble service.[4]

As a disciple, Peter saw Jesus' miracles up close. One of the most amazing was the time when Jesus walked on water. Then Jesus called Peter to walk on the water as well, and for a moment he succeeded. Matthew 14:30 (KJV) tells us what happened next: "When he [Peter] saw the wind boisterous, he was afraid; and beginning to sink, he cried, saying, Lord, save me." Though Peter had seen with his own eyes what Jesus could do, he lost his faith momentarily. Of course, the Lord rescued Peter. Jesus knew that even with all that Peter had experienced and seen, he still had some growing to do in his spiritual life.

That wasn't Peter's only failure. Many times throughout the Gospels, we read of occasions when Peter reasoned more with his heart than with his brain. He went with his emotions more than he should have, and he even hurt the Lord with his careless words. Remember what happened just before the Lord brought Peter, James, and John to the Mount of Transfiguration? The Lord was beginning to share with His disciples what would happen to Him in Jerusalem. He explained that soon He would be rejected and crucified, but that afterward He would rise again. Peter began to rebuke the Lord, saying that none of this was going to happen. Peter said this because of his great love for the Lord and because He didn't want to see the Lord hurt. Yet Jesus strongly rebuked Peter. He told Peter not to take His words lightly, for they were words from God.

M. R. DeHaan, radio teacher and writer, said about this passage, "Now, this strange answer of Jesus, in turning to Peter and rebuking the devil, is a marvelous picture of the indescribable, unfathomable love and grace of the Savior. The Lord understood the struggle within Simon Peter's heart, the two voices that battled for expression. . . . We might have expected our Lord to disown Peter entirely. But Jesus does nothing of the kind. He simply reminds Peter that the flesh is still with him, and in a moment of confidence, he was able to fall."[5]

Commentator J. C. Ryle said, "Peter's eyes were blinded to the necessity of our Lord's death. He actually did what he could to prevent that death taking place at all!"[6] With all of his mistakes, I'm sure there were times when Peter wondered if he would ever make it as a disciple.

Maybe you have felt that way about something you tried to learn, whether it was a new program on a computer, a different position at work, or a different recipe for the family dinner. Even though you did everything possible to learn a new skill, you found it more difficult than you thought it would be. It is easy to feel this way when you face something new and unfamiliar. Maybe you've had times when you've thought that no matter how hard you tried, your effort just wasn't good enough. I once heard about a toy designed to teach children about the computer age that was so complicated no one could ever assemble it. Imagine how children would feel about a toy they can't figure out. They would think that they lack the intelligence and ability. I'm sure Peter felt this way about his own calling to be a disciple.

Peter especially failed when he said strongly that he wouldn't fail. It is interesting to note that just when Peter *thought* he couldn't fail, he *did* fail. This is the opposite of most of what is heard about "positive thinking" today. Peter really believed that he would never let down his Lord, but he was wrong. So "positive thinking" isn't the solution we need.

On that tragic night before Jesus' crucifixion, Peter abandoned the Lord first by falling asleep in the Garden of Gethsemane. His physical weariness overcame his desire to stay awake. Later, when Jesus was brought to trial, Peter denied three times that he even knew Jesus. He denied his faith and his Lord, although just days before that, he had said that he would never deny Him!

Peter's failure here was no small thing. He denied Jesus not once but three times. These denials weren't mere whispers; Mark tells us that in the third denial, Peter called down curses upon himself (Mark 14:71). Very few of the events in Jesus' life are repeated in all four Gospels; Peter's denial appears in all four. When Peter failed, he failed big time!

Yet as we look back on Peter's life, we don't consider him a failure, do we? Have you ever heard one Bible teacher say that Peter was a failure? Have you ever read a book that stated that this disciple was a failure? He isn't considered a failure; he is said to be one of the greatest of the apostles.

Jesus knew Peter's grief and sorrow. After Jesus rose from the dead, He wanted to make sure that Peter knew He still loved him and cared about him. When Jesus spoke to the women who had come to visit His tomb, He told them to tell the disciples *and Peter* that He had risen from the dead (Mark 16:7). He specifically mentioned Peter by name. What's more, Jesus made His forgiveness abundantly clear when He called Peter to feed His sheep (John 21:15-19). By "sheep" Jesus meant those who were going to trust in Him as their Savior. In other words, Jesus was giving Peter the responsibility of spiritually feeding and nurturing other believers. He gave Peter a position of authority even though He knew Peter's weaknesses. That's because Jesus loves those who are His own.

A Love That Never Ceases

Do you know that the Lord feels the same way about you? Whether you fail in a small way or a huge way, He will never stop loving you. Jesus showed His love for you by giving the ultimate sacrifice for you; His death on the cross paid the penalty for your sins. Before Jesus Christ died on the cross, your sins separated you from God. If you died in your natural, unregenerated state, your penalty would be hell.

But God in His great love (John 3:16) reached out to you by sending His beloved Son. Because Jesus lived a perfect life, He was able to pay the penalty that you would have had to pay. Jesus loves you so much He was willing to die so that you might have eternal life. There is no better proof of Jesus' love for you than that. If Jesus' love can transcend all of your sins, then you can know with certainty that His love will transcend all your mistakes.

Now Peter could have chosen to sulk over his mistakes, but he didn't. Peter didn't remain a failure because he didn't quit. He didn't let his own mistakes become stumbling blocks. Instead, he used them as stepping-stones by admitting his faults and then going on, humbled by the experience. He was excited that God cared about him enough to never leave him nor forsake him.

Peter was a piece of clay who, by the end of his life, turned into granite. In fact, it didn't take long for God to begin ministering through Peter in mighty ways. Just a few weeks after denying Jesus, Peter preached a powerful sermon on the day of Pentecost that jump-started the church by bringing thousands of people to trust Christ as their Savior.

Learning from Peter's Example

We can all learn from Peter's example. His eagerness and zeal for the things of God should be an encouragement to us. And his failures can actually inspire us to achieve great things for the Lord Jesus Christ. Peter didn't quit even though there were times in his life when he might have felt entitled to do just that. Instead, his failures presented an opportunity for him to learn more about himself so he could become more like his Lord.

Friend, as you struggle in this world of antibiblical values and expectations, there are times when you are going to be discouraged. Sometimes you will look at your own failings and think that maybe God can't use you. Maybe you are aching to feel the presence of God in your life, but for some reason you think your prayers are not getting past the ceiling. You feel as if God has abandoned you!

But God never abandons His own. He loves us even in the midst of our failures. Remember this: God used Peter in spite of his sins. In fact, it was those times in which Peter had failed that he realized where his strength really lay. Instead of letting his failures become an obstacle, he allowed them to drive him closer to God and to yield to God's powerful influence in his life.

What about you? Are you willing to be encouraged by the example of this man of God? You too can find this wonderful truth when you take off the disguise of failure and realize that hidden underneath is a great opportunity to expect God's hand of blessing in your life.

2

THE TOWEL, THE WAY TO THE THRONE

GOLF PRO HARVEY PENICK'S greatest success came late in his career. He is best known for his "little books" on golf. Yet Penick never wrote with the intention of making money. In the 1920s he purchased a red spiral notebook in which he recorded his observations on golf. He kept this notebook for decades. In 1991 he showed it to a writer and asked if he thought it was worth publishing. The writer agreed to help him find a publisher. A short time later the man sent Penick a letter telling him that Simon and Schuster had agreed to an advance of $90,000.

This news didn't seem to bring much joy to Penick. He told his writer friend that with all his medical bills, there was no way he could advance the publishing house that much money. The writer then explained that Penick would *receive* the $90,000! The book was titled *Harvey Penick's Little Red Book*, and it sold more than a million copies.[1]

Penick's attitude wasn't, "I've written a great book. It deserves to sell." His humble attitude should be the outlook of the servant of God. Even with all the instruction in the Scriptures on pride, the people of God tend to think of ministry not in terms of how they can *serve* but in terms of how they can *be served*.

Pride is one of the most dangerous and sinister of sins. Writer David Rhodes said, "Pride is a dandelion of the soul. Its roots go deep and if only a little is left, it will sprout again. The danger of pride is that it feeds on goodness." Most people wish to serve God, but they tend to do so in an advisory capacity rather than with a faithful servant's heart.

It isn't hard to deduce from reading about Peter in the Bible that his main problem was pride. Someone said that pride is the only disease that makes everyone sick except the person who has it.

If a person wanted an important position in a kingdom, he probably wouldn't seek it by cleaning out the moat around the castle! He would make sure he knew the right people and had enough money to make the right connections. He would strategically plan each political move in order to make the highest advancement. But the real way to the throne is much different from what most people think. Peter found this out.

There are those of us who would look at Peter's life and think, *That man had so much pride he could never be used of God!* The Lord had quite a different take on Peter's life. He saw a seed of servanthood hidden behind the insidious mass of pride in Peter's heart. And with his divine surgeon's knife, He began to cut away all that was in the way of that servanthood.

God knew that Peter would be willing to change once he was shown the truth. The patient has to first be willing to go to the doctor for diagnosis and then be willing to face the solution, which might be an extensive operation. If the patient isn't willing, then there is no cure. Peter had a trait that all of us need to cultivate—a willingness to change those things in his life that kept him from having a servant's heart.

There are those of us in Christian service who are so set in what we do that when the Lord shows us something we need to change, we find ourselves unwilling. The familiar seems safer. We don't subject ourselves to divine surgery. Instead, we hang back, unwilling to give ourselves the chance to become more like the Lord.

Settling into this thought pattern is dangerous. Essentially we are telling the Lord, "I don't need to change anymore. I'm safe doing what I am doing now."

The *Telegraph Journal* reported that a tractor-trailer truck flipped over on a Canadian highway. Traffic stopped while firefighters spread peat moss to soak up the spilled diesel fuel. A brief torrential rain washed most of the gardening material away, so they sent for more. Caught up in the moment, no one noticed that the cargo in the overturned trailer *was* peat moss. The solution to the problem was right in front of the firefighters, but they didn't realize it.

And so it is in our own lives. The solution lies in the Word of God, but many times we don't want to accept it. As we begin our study on some of the key events in the life of the apostle Peter, we see the solution to his pride kneeling at his feet, towel in hand.

The Servant Solution

> *He riseth from supper, and laid aside his garments; and took a towel, and girded himself. After that he poureth water into a basin, and began to wash the disciples' feet, and to wipe them with the towel wherewith he was girded.*
>
> *Then cometh he to Simon Peter: and Peter saith unto him, Lord, dost thou wash my feet? Jesus answered and said unto him, What I do thou knowest not now; but thou shalt know hereafter. Peter saith unto him, Thou shalt never wash my feet. Jesus answered him, If I wash thee not, thou hast no part with me. Simon Peter saith unto him, Lord, not my feet only, but also my hands and my head. (John 13:4-9)*

Think about the setting. A small room. Dirty, sweaty disciples who had just walked the dusty streets of Jerusalem. And no servant to do the necessary Middle Eastern custom of washing everyone's feet. This was before the days of showers!

Then the Lord of glory steps forward, girds Himself as a servant, and washes each disciple's feet—to the utter astonishment of all and probably some chagrin because none of them had been willing to do the task. The Midrash taught that no Hebrew, even a slave, could be commanded to wash feet.[2]

Peter's reaction was anger. Seeing the Lord perform such a menial task confounded his view of a triumphant Messiah. He believed that Jesus was God, sent in human flesh. Yet this God who created the universe with His hands was using those same hands to wash his feet. No one would expect someone like Michael Jordan to clean up the locker room after an NBA championship; that job would be considered too lowly for the great basketball player.

And in the same way, Peter didn't want a servant Jesus who cleaned up locker rooms; he wanted a strong Jesus who would overturn Rome. Jesus has again taken the high road by doing the lowly task. He didn't fit into Peter's kingly mold.

All of us are guilty of thinking what Peter thought, trying to make the Lord and His will for our lives into what we think He and it should be. We think we can control our own and everyone else's problems, even though we know that role belongs to God. We act as if we know what God would do even though we act without His sanction. At times we try to create things out of nothing, even trying to be other people's savior.

Thinking Jesus should perform in a certain manner was one of the things Peter needed to relinquish. He finally realized a critical truth. Jesus' plan for Peter was far more important than the plan Peter wanted for his life. Peter would later write, "Casting all your care upon him; for he careth for you,"[3] in the book of 1 Peter. However at the moment of the foot-washing, Peter didn't know what it meant to depend on the Lord.

Do you sometimes want to take control out of the Lord's hands, tired of waiting for the Lord's answer to your problem? Maybe you think you have waited long enough for a reply. Yet that thought parallels Peter's blunder, wanting to be in control of his life, rather than yielding to God's control and finding the greater life Christ had for him.

We easily fall into this trap. A single mom can really relate to this feeling. A bad first marriage leaves her trying to pick up the pieces of her life, not to mention the lives of her children. Often she feels overwhelmed by the pressures she faces day in and day out from parenting, and in addition she wants to meet someone who can satisfy her longings for companionship. Struggling to cope, she easily begins to doubt the Lord's provision.

It seems to be taking an interminably long period of time for someone to come into her life. The men she meets are not godly examples. The temptation is strong after a while to look past those worldly characteristics and latch onto someone, knowing full well that person isn't the one God would have for her. She may not even realize the gradual shift of her priorities until she is irrevocably married into even more heartaches than before.

We have all been guilty of taking matters into our own hands when it comes to dealing with a difficult situation, thinking that if we sit back and wait on God, nothing is going to happen. Yet the lesson Peter learned from having to sit back and let the Lord wash his feet is invaluable to us as Christians. If you are contemplating a change in your relationships, your job, education, or any given situation, a good rule of thumb is: Don't latch on to the easy solution unless you are *sure* the solution is from God. Peter needed to learn that it was Jesus, not Peter, who was in control. That is just the lesson God is trying to teach us.

Peter's desire for control reminds me of my son as a baby. He hated the wind, and when it blew against his face, he would blow back as hard as he could. He seemed to think that he could control what the wind was doing by blowing back at it.

This need for our own control reminds me of a story told by a Filipino pastor. The carabao driver was on his way to market when he overtook an old man carrying a heavy load. Taking compassion on him, the driver invited the old man to ride in the wagon. Gratefully the man accepted. After a few minutes, the driver turned to see how the man was doing. To his surprise, he found his passenger sitting in the wagon but still straining under the heavy weight, for he had not taken the burden off his shoulders.

Placing our burden on the Lord's shoulders means that we finally experience rest. Realize that you may never learn the *reason* why you are facing your current problem. When we look past the unfair circumstances and trust in the Lord's overwhelming goodness, we begin to emerge from our confusion, and we find peace.

Self-righteous Service Is Not True Service

Peter's first question, "Lord, are you going to wash my feet?" shows his attitude toward the Lord's actions. Did Peter expect Jesus to wash all the disciples' feet and not wash his? As usual Peter used this question as a conversation starter so he could get to the point he wanted to make. "Lord, You will never wash my feet," he said boldly, feeling proud of his humble statement.

There was an ulterior motive in his declaration. He was really saying, "Lord, why are You doing this lowly job? Don't wash my feet! Get up, and put on Your crown! Call up Your entourage of chariots and perform Your kingly duties."

The true mark of a spiritual man or woman is the desire to do any job, no matter how "lowly." During the American Revolution, a man in civilian clothes rode past a group of soldiers repairing a small defensive barrier. Their leader was shouting instructions, but he was not attempting to help them. Asked why by the rider, he retorted with great dignity, "Sir, I am a corporal!" The stranger apologized, dismounted, and proceeded to help the exhausted soldiers. The job done, he turned to the corporal and said, "Mr. Corporal, next time you have a job like this and not enough men to do it, go to your commander-in-chief, and I will come and help you again." It was none other than George Washington.[4]

Washington showed his greatness by being willing to do a menial job. The Lord Jesus showed His supreme power by His simple act of service. Even though Peter didn't think the Lord should do such a task, the disciple's attitude didn't deter the Lord.

Consider for a moment your own attitude toward servanthood. How would you feel if your pastor asked you to clean the bathrooms at church or help with a youth group event? Would his request make you feel that he doesn't appreciate your true worth? Or would you agree wholeheartedly, realizing that the opportunity to serve is a privilege?

Think back on the past few months of your service to your church and community. In what ways have you served others? It is important to determine whether you are serving with grace or with greed. I've included a series of questions that can help you determine the motivation behind your service.

1) Do you expect other church members to praise your service to Christ? Or are you satisfied if your service pleases God?

2) Does your service come from gratitude to the Lord? Or are you motivated because other people will thank you for what you do?

3) Are you self-righteous as you work in the church, expecting others to do their service the exact way you do? Or are you content to do the "big things" and "little things" just because they give you an opportunity to show how much you love the Lord?

4) Do you expect prosperity because you serve? Or are you content even if no one finds out?

5) Do you employ "selective service," deciding who and when you will serve? Or do you help anyone, thanking God for the privilege?

6) Do you serve only when you "feel" like it? Or do you serve when you are called?

7) Are you always looking for a "better" position, one that will showcase your talents? Or are you content, realizing that service is a part of your life?

This test helps determine the level of our commitment. None of us could answer yes to the second question in each pair every day of the week! Rather, the questions reflect a progression. One or two good answers mean it is time to reevaluate your dedication to serve. Four to six good answers mean you are on the right track!

Take a snapshot in your mind of Christ washing the disciples' feet and use that as your litmus test when you perform your own service toward others. *Self-sacrificing*, not *self-righteous*, service is an essential part of the formula for spiritual success. Learning to do acts of service even when they aren't recognized or rewarded is probably the most difficult lesson for the Christian to learn. Yet this is necessary for our attitude to be right as we serve in the home, the church, and the world.

The Biggest Piece of Cake

It was my granddaughter Erica's birthday. The cake sat in all its glory in the middle of the table. Seven candles were lit, and Erica took a deep breath, ready to blow them out when a fight broke out between Jamie (my five-year-old grandson) and Amanda (my two-year-old granddaughter).

"I want the biggest piece!" Jamie said.

"No. Mine," Amanda countered.

While an argument over the biggest piece of cake is cute between children, the attitude of wanting the biggest share shouldn't characterize the servant of God. Too many times this is what happens in Christian circles, in the church, and especially in individuals.

In the book of Matthew we see that toward the end of Jesus' ministry, an ugly competitive spirit developed among the apostles.

James, John, and their mother attempted to get Jesus to promise them privileged thrones in the kingdom.[5] Just after this, Jesus called them all together and said, "But it shall not be so among you: but whosoever will be great among you, let him be your minister; And whosoever will be chief among you, let him be your servant: Even as the Son of man came not to be ministered unto, but to minister, and to give his life a ransom for many" (Matthew 20:26-28).

Our acts parallel those of the disciples at times. Cloaking our ambitious plans for self in a spiritual mantle, we might say, "I appreciate the offer to help in a Sunday school class of two-year-olds, but I feel it would be a better use of my talents if I taught the adults." Teaching the adult Sunday school would be an act of service, but the teacher can practically be guaranteed more appreciation from the grownups than from the kids!

Robert Raines summed up the situation in the following poem:

I am like James and John.
Lord, I size up other people
In terms of what they can do for me;
How they can further my program,
feed my ego,
satisfy my needs,
give me strategic advantage.
I exploit people,
  ostensibly for your sake,
  but really for my own sake.
Lord, I turn to you
  to get the inside track
  and obtain special favors,
  your direction for my schemes,
  your power for my projects,
  your sanction for my ambitions,
  your blank checks for whatever I want.
I am like James and John.[6]

Think again about your motivation for service. Do you do the things you do because of the affirming praise you receive or because you desire to please the Lord? When Christ performed the menial task of washing the disciples' feet, He showed us so much about our true motivation. He was willing to do both the lowly jobs and the important jobs with enthusiasm and with fervor. Make this same commitment. We can't be perfect in this, for even we ourselves don't know our hearts. But we can begin to perform those lowly acts of service and follow His great example. Doing so shifts our focus from what we receive to what we can give. And there is no better definition of a servant than that.

The towel you hold in your hand to do this service might feel like rough cotton. And yet when that towel is used in His name, it is made of the most sumptuous cloth, fit only to lay at His feet. Decide today that the way to the throne begins with the towel.

Choosing to Serve Even When It Hurts

Later when Peter reflected on the events of that day and night before the crucifixion, many things would become clear. He would begin to understand that every word, every action, every remark, and every thought Christ had all combined into a glorious tapestry of service. It would take many years for him to understand the events of that fateful night. But he learned one thing right away. In the midst of His most intense pain, the Lord chose to serve others.

As I've faced deep trials, I have begun to comprehend this truth. When I am in the deepest pain, I need to be in the deepest service. If anyone had a right to a pity party, it was the Lord. Yet we see that humility is the key to handling great pressure. Instead of giving in to His feelings of grief, He chose an act of self-sacrifice.

It is the same way in our own lives. When the shut-in feels the worst—not just because of the pain she has to endure but due to her isolation from the outside world—she is understandably prone to discouragement and despair. Besides the nurse who gives her care, she has very little contact with other people and begins to feel depressed and anxious because of her inability to contribute to others as she did in the past.

A dear saint who faced this kind of situation wrote me a letter. She had ministered in her church for many years, but now due to health problems she finds herself cooped up in her home. On occasion some relatives bring dinner, and a hired nurse takes care of most of her needs. But for the most part she is alone. Depression was beginning to overwhelm this woman so used to taking care of others. One day while watching our TV broadcast, she heard me say how important the ministry of prayer was. I mentioned that if all you can do is lie in bed, maybe God is calling you to prayer. She began keeping a list of things to pray about—her church concerns, her family worries, and mission projects—and carved out a structured time to pray for those needs each day.

In her letter to me she explained how her joy has begun to return because once again she feels useful in the body of Christ. She has found an important secret. In times of distress or pain, service to Him in any form will bring renewal and hope.

Are you facing the trial of a new job, sick family members, or difficult relationships? Instead of giving in to pity, why not choose to serve? Maybe the church bulletins need collating, or maintenance is required on the church grounds. When you choose service, you are guaranteed that you are following behind Christ as He stooped down, picked up a basin of water, and washed the disciples' feet. When your dreams are shattered, don't throw in the towel; *get the towel* and start doing acts of service.

You Might Get Kicked in the Face

Once Winston Churchill was sitting on a platform waiting to speak to a large crowd gathered to hear him. The chairman of the event leaned over and said, "Isn't it exciting, Mr. Churchill, that all these people came just to hear you speak?"

Churchill responded, "It is quite flattering, but whenever I feel this way, I always remember that if instead of making a political speech I was being hanged, the crowd would be twice as big." Churchill had a proper perspective on himself. It is even more necessary for the servant of God to have the biblical perspective of himself. D. L. Moody said, "Be humble or you will stumble," and this phrase is an easy way for the believer to remember what God expects.

Outside my sun porch I have set up several bird feeders. The highlight of my day is having my devotional time while gazing at God's grand creation, the birds. I've noticed that each bird has a different personality. Some are more likely to let other birds perch at the feeder. Others, like the blue jays, want the whole feeder to themselves when they choose to grace it with their presence. Their electric blue feathers light up the area around the feeder, but their personality matches their coloring. Bold and brash, these birds seem to think they are stronger than eagles and the crowning achievement of beauty.

I've noticed another bird that is just as beautiful, but he doesn't seem to flaunt it. The cardinals perch on the feeder with any bird, even the lowly sparrow. They don't seem to have the same opinion of themselves as the blue jays.

Peter and the rest of the disciples were acting like noisy blue jays, each of them wanting to flaunt his own splendor, while the Lord Jesus was acting more gentle than even a cardinal. Like the mildest of peaceful doves, the Lord Jesus showed them in living color that the way to the throne was through an act of service.

As the Lord Jesus knelt in front of each disciple (even Judas!), He was showing His vulnerability. He was opening himself up to being kicked in the face as He went one by one with the basin and towel. And the parallel can be drawn to our own acts of service.

True service for Christ opens us up to being kicked in the face. Our motives can be misinterpreted. Our actual act of service can be misunderstood. When this happens, it is tempting to say, "Every time I try to do something for the Lord, I get hurt in some way. That's it. I'm through." But we don't see the Lord stop even at Judas as He washed each disciple's feet. He showed us that He cared only about one thing, and that is what God thought of Him. When we truly serve, we will do the same.

Walking Daily with Christ

There are many lessons we can draw from the account of the foot-washing, but perhaps one of the most important is a vital truth about the Christian's daily walk. Jesus showed the disciples and all Christians who would follow Him that a spiritual foot-washing would be necessary for fellowship: "Peter saith unto him, Thou shalt never wash my feet. Jesus answered him, If I wash thee not, thou hast no part with me. Simon Peter saith unto him, Lord, not my feet only, but also my hands and my head" (John 13:8-9).

This word *part* is used in terms of fellowship with Christ. Christ said that if Peter did not allow Him to wash his feet, then he could have no fellowship with Christ. Jesus meant this in a spiritual sense.

Our flesh and the world are like the dusty roads of Israel. As we live each day, we are bound to be soiled by this worldly system. Remember 1 John 1:9: "If we confess our sins, he is faithful and just to forgive us our sins, and to cleanse us from all unrighteousness." By daily confessing our sins to Christ, we are able to continue serving because of His "foot-washing."

There is a "one-time bath" that cleanses you the moment you trust Christ as your Savior. When Jesus died on the cross, He paid the penalty for your sins—past, present, and future. When you trust in the payment He made, His blood cleanses you from head to toe.

However, the foot-washing was to show the disciples that it was possible to walk daily with Christ. As they evangelized the world after Jesus' resurrection, they remembered that lesson in the Upper Room. When they sinned, they were able to restore their fellowship with Christ by confessing that sin.

Take a minute and think about your life. Do you go to Christ daily, hold out your dusty soul stained and soiled by sin, and ask Him to wash it? Making this a practice will give you daily communion with Christ that will delight your soul.

Strength for a Lifetime

When the believer goes to the Lord daily for his spiritual "foot-washing," he then discovers another secret to living the Christian life. Those times of confession can be the beginning of a daily quiet time with your Bible, a time when you sit down with the Word of God and read a portion of it. Not only will the spiritual discipline further your walk with Christ, but it will also force you to tell Him your concerns and fears. Taking time for Bible study and prayer gives the Lord a chance to work.

Just as Peter needed to learn that the Lord wanted him to relax, so I think that many Christians would find peace and strength in stopping for a moment in the midst of their busy service. Your attitude will change as you understand a vital truth. Until you become filled with the Lord's strength, you won't have the strength to address other people's spiritual needs. Until you take time to meditate on the promises of God, you won't be able to share those promises with others.

After spending personal time with the Lord, you will find strength where before you didn't have the stamina to do those menial tasks for Him. Where you were once powerless, now you have the power. Where you once didn't even desire the task, now you have the will to do even those lowly acts of service. When you allow the Lord to wash your feet, you will then have the strength to wash others' feet.

The strength you receive from our Savior is the secret to the Christian life. This prayerful time alone with God will give you strength to last a lifetime in strong, spiritual service.

Slow and Steady Wins the Race

Just as quickly as Peter's pride popped up, so did the tender side of his nature. For Peter wanted fellowship with Christ more than anything else. One thing for sure, Peter needed his feet to be clean because he had them in his mouth so much of the time!

Peter quickly backed down from his first prideful statement: "Lord, you aren't going to wash my feet." His tune changed to: "Lord, wash any part of me You want!" and I admire this. When the rebuke was given, Peter quickly surrendered his own pride. One writer called him impetuous, blustering, blundering, spouting Simon Peter! What an unpredictable disciple he was, and yet withal, we cannot help but love him at least for his frankness and bluntness, for one always knew where Simon Peter stood.[7]

I have rebuked people, and they refused to admit they were wrong. Others I have taken aside and noticed immediately a wonderful spirit as they realized their mistake, confessed it, and were able to serve in even greater fashion than before. This characteristic was one of the reasons the Lord was able to work with Peter. He admitted his fault and was willing to change.

The Lord patiently worked with Peter to make him like gold. Peter showed how much the Lord had changed him when he stood to preach on the day of Pentecost. Those assembled were amazed most of all by Peter's eloquence and passion. Filled with the Spirit's power, his preaching spurred thousands to trust in Jesus Christ.

Peter needed this preparation by Christ. He needed to see Christ wash the disciples' feet. He needed to see those acts of service that Christ performed in spite of His deep pain. It was almost time for Peter to emerge and lead the church, but there were a few final lessons he needed to learn.

In an article in *Pastoral Renewal*, Charles Simpson wrote that he knew a young man who dove for exotic fish for aquariums. He said that one of the most popular aquarium fish is the shark. If you catch a small shark and confine it, it will stay a size proportionate to the aquarium. Sharks can be six inches long yet fully matured. However, if you turn them loose in the ocean, they grow to their normal length of eight feet. Simpson furthers this analogy by saying that he has seen this happen to some Christians. He has seen the cutest little six-inch Christians who swim around in a puddle. But if you put them into a larger arena—into the whole creation—only then can they become great.[8]

Peter needed the small aquarium of the twelve disciples and the constant care of the Lord in order to be launched into the world.

When two of my granddaughters were small, they wanted me to play house with them. My oldest, Amy, said, "Papa, we want you to be the baby."

"How do I act like a baby?" I asked.

"You need to cry."

I pretended to cry. Amy interrupted me, "Papa, you are not a good baby. Go to your room!"

Do you ever feel as if you are being sent to your room because you aren't ministering to as many people as you would like? Perhaps you held a position of prominence, but now you have a less elevated rank. As you study the life of Peter, you will see how this time "in his room" enabled him to develop to his full potential for the Lord.

This truth will encourage you to continue serving no matter what task the Lord has given you, because it is in this time of confinement that He will do His greatest work in your life.

SUCCESS EQUALS SERVICE

Our Lord's example in washing the disciples' feet teaches us many things about how the Christian should perceive spiritual success. Jesus made it clear that success is not found in the Cadillac driving toward the kingdom but in a simple act of service. It is not found in reaching, but in kneeling. Servanthood equals spiritual success. While this definition is contrary to the world's view, it is crucial that the believer practice a servant attitude in his or her daily life. For when we open ourselves up to possibly being kicked in the face as a result of our service, it is then that we capture the spirit of what Christ meant when He said, "Inasmuch as ye have done it unto one of the least of these my brethren, ye have done it unto me" (Matthew 25:40).

3

Peter Says the Wrong Thing the Right Way

MARRIED FIFTEEN YEARS, Mary and Gene's relationship was mainly one of love and trust. Yet in the heat of an argument once, Gene said to Mary, "I wish I had never married you." When he tried to apologize, he realized he could never take those words back.

Andrew's boss called him into the office for his six-month review. He told Andrew that he was taking too much personal time. Although Andrew knew this was true, he proceeded to "tell his boss off," ruining his chances of promotion.

Marisa felt frustrated when she saw Samuel's report card. "You are my biggest disappointment," she said, immediately feeling sorry when she saw her son's expression.

I'm sure you have witnessed firsthand the havoc caused by one foolhardy statement. Political figures, sports celebrities, and business leaders have hindered if not ruined their careers with one thoughtless remark. Spouses, single parents, and siblings damage their relationships in one moment of rudeness. Throughout the years, people have said to me that their most vivid memory from childhood was a cruel thing one of their parents said. Those words might be forgiven, but they are almost impossible to forget. All of us sometimes forget the dynamic power words hold. Remember that there is only a single letter's difference between words and swords.

Once there lived an imaginary lady who is related to all of us at times. Her name is Iva Footen-Mouth. She told her husband,

Henry, "All I said was that Mrs. Smith's boys are the most demanding in my class. Never mind that their dad lost his job and is suffering from depression. I realize Mrs. Smith has had to work two jobs to make ends meet. And of course, Henry, I realize she *heard* me complaining about her bratty kids! But remember the Scripture says to "lie not."[1]

This humorous example shows that sometimes we stoop to use Scripture to justify our damaging words. Mrs. Footen-Mouth forgot to mention another important passage that tells us to speak words that minister grace![2]

A passage in Mark 14 highlights this tendency in Peter: "And Jesus saith unto them, All ye shall be offended because of me this night: for it is written, I will smite the shepherd, and the sheep shall be scattered. But after that I am risen, I will go before you into Galilee. But Peter said unto him, Although all shall be offended, yet will not I" (Mark 14:27-29).

Looking ahead to the events at the trial of Jesus, we see that not only was Peter offended because of Christ, but he also denied his Lord three times. "And the second time the cock crew. And Peter called to mind the word that Jesus said unto him, Before the cock crow twice, thou shalt deny me thrice. And when he thought thereon, he wept" (Mark 14:72).

The apostle Peter's last name could have been Footen-Mouth! He knew what it was to say brash things and regret them. This tendency is recorded several times throughout the Gospels. Some passages to study further are Matthew 14:29; 16:22-23 and John 13:36-37; 18:27.

Everyone is susceptible to the occasional faux pas, but for some people saying the wrong thing is the rule rather than the exception. These individuals are sometimes leader-type personalities and are also gregarious and open. However, hurtful words tumble out of their mouths as quickly as positive ones.

Most of Peter's brash statements were made on the heel of

remarkable testimonials about his devotion to the Lord. Washington Irving said, "A sharp tongue is the only edged tool that grows keener with constant use." Peter's big heart is evident in his declarations of faith in the Lord, and maybe this was what he counted on to overcome the effects of his quick tongue. This is why if you read only *part* of the Gospels, you would come to the conclusion that Peter was a failure. He thought his love for God would be enough. What he did not realize was the insufficiency of his own strength.

I am sure you have experienced the same thing. Maybe you went to a church service or seminar and learned some godly principles, only to go to work on Monday and become frustrated at your boss. Instead of applying the guidelines you had learned, you expressed your anger in a negative way. Maybe you determined to be patient with your children, only to find yourself "flying off the handle" the next time they provoked each other. Possibly you were inspired to share your faith, only to find the supermarket clerk's rebuff too difficult to handle. While you desired to do the right thing, your own flesh got in the way and kept you from it. In looking at the life of the apostle, we see a paradox of goodness and brashness. We see a fervent leader and a fumbling follower, a spiritual giant and faltering bystander, an outspoken witness and an uncertain onlooker.

I know God has called me to do what I am doing. I enjoy preaching and running a ministry. Yet in the hard times I come to the sobering realization that only God's power enables me to move forward. In moments of doubt, I find myself, like Peter, having to realize that everything is God's, and I am simply an instrument in His hand. We are all in the same boat as Peter sometimes.

Detour Next Ten Miles

It is important to realize that Peter's denial of Christ, cursing the servant girl, etc., did not bring him to maturity, but God's conviction did. When Peter realized his terrible sin and the magnitude of the Lord's love and grace as Christ sought him out after the resurrection, these understandings brought him to maturity. Sin always pulls us away from God. It is the chastening, contrition, and confession that bring us back and can make us better Christians. Certainly it would have been better for Peter not to sin. Yet the disciple learned that when he did sin, it was because of a weakness he needed to change.

Many failures, of course, do not involve sin at all. Sometimes those failures can be described as detours on the road of life. Think about a vacation. The kids are finally in the car, and after what seems like a hundred songs and jokes, they fall asleep. Exhausted from packing, you and your spouse are overjoyed to be on your way. Both of you have been counting on this break to spend quality time together as a couple and as a family. Pulling out on the interstate, you set the cruise control to sixty-five and lean back. Finally you can relax! Then a sign looms ahead: Detour Next Ten Miles. What a pain! Just when you thought you could unwind, you have to change your plans.

Think about your journey on the spiritual expressway. What happens when you are set on cruise control and unexpectedly come to that aggravating detour? How do you react? And after you have taken it, do you realize that the detour brought you an opportunity to draw closer to Christ?

A Bible from my college days bears the following handwritten inscription next to a passage in the Psalms: "Here I sit at Brinks, not knowing where to go, not knowing what to do, but God will take care." I enjoyed working at Brinks, a company that picks up and delivers money from businesses, while I attended school. It was a great job because I was able to study while I was working. However, a bypass in the road brought me fresh appreciation for my Lord's provision and my job.

Knowing that I needed to study while on the job, the supervisor had promised me a position inside. However, since the school semester didn't start for a few months, I was assigned the task of transferring the moneyboxes from Miami transit buses to a vault. It was hot, thankless work. The exhaust from the buses covered me with grime. I did this work hour after hour, knowing that in a few months, I would be doing something else.

When the semester was about to start, I approached my boss and said, "I'm ready to start my inside job."

He replied, "I'm sorry, but you need to continue to work outside." Disappointed I said, "I guess I can't work here then."

I found another job and began my first day. It was discouraging because I realized I couldn't study in this position either. Then I got a call from Brinks. A new position was open, and I would be able to work inside if I would return. I met with my current boss, and he said he totally understood why I needed to go back to Brinks. So I went back. That is when I penned those lines on the margin next to Psalm 37:4: "Delight thyself also in the Lord; and he shall give thee the desires of thine heart."

Why did I experience that detour? The experience was a powerful reminder that I needed to depend on God. I realized that while God might allow the devil to give us a detour in life's freeway, our enemy can't stop us from reaching our final destination. The indirect route I took made me realize anew that only through trials could I really grow.

This was true in Peter's life. It was in the tough times when he keenly felt his own failings that he matured into a strong leader. Our inadequacies shouldn't steer us toward self-pity. Instead, they should drive us to the place we should never have left—our knees. In prayer alone with God, we will experience His love and power. We will realize that His plan for our lives is far better than our own.

Woodrow Kroll explains about true closeness with God: "It is much easier to find intimacy with God if you do not see yourself as wandering alone along the interstate, deep into the night, without a clue which direction you should go. Instead, see yourself as one loved by God—loved so much He sent His Son to die for you."[3]

Perhaps you are feeling inadequate in your Christian life. Take heart. As God greatly used Peter, so He will use you. Whether you are at a place of faith or fear, through God's workmanship you will be fashioned into a beautiful masterpiece of great use to Him.

Powerful Potential

Peter's potential could be compared to that of a dormant seed. A harsh outer shell covered his budding greatness. The times he said the wrong thing, the times he failed the Lord—those were the catalysts that made him realize he needed to change. After the resurrection of Christ from the dead, Peter would stand before a huge multitude and preach a stirring message. "But Peter, standing up with the eleven, lifted up his voice, and said unto them, Ye men of Judaea, and all ye that dwell at Jerusalem, be this known unto you, and hearken to my words" (Acts 2:14). The sermon continues throughout the second chapter. As a result of Peter's preaching, over 3,000 souls were saved! Imagine being able to see that many people come to Christ!

The late cartoonist Charles M. Schulz said, "There is no greater burden than great potential." I think Peter knew he could be a great leader when he first followed Christ. This is why he was always willing to jump into the water, make the brash statement, or declare the groundbreaking confession of faith.

Maybe you have recently moved into a challenging situation. Perhaps you thought you could handle a different position at work, only to find yourself floundering. Maybe you have decided to stay within a budget for your family but are finding it difficult to buy the groceries and other items you need on a daily basis. Possibly the new position you received has been hard on your family. You didn't realize how much extra time this job would take. All of us have a tendency to leap before we look.

So if you have made a mistake, does this mean you should quit? Because you are in a bad situation that is your fault, are you a failure? It is important to remember that you aren't a failure even if you have failed. Peter's blunders didn't make him a failure, and neither do yours. If you've made a mistake by taking a difficult job, then go ahead and get the needed training. Don't be afraid to try new things. If your budget isn't working for you, go ahead, look through it, and make the required adjustments toward becoming a good steward. Don't let a failure keep you from continuing the race.

Love That Has No Limits

In spite of Peter's shortcomings, we see the picture of the ever-patient and loving Lord. He rebuked Peter when he needed it, but Christ's love and concern for Peter were visible and real. The Lord used the disciple's stumbling words to remind him of his humanness. Mark 14:30 states, "And Jesus saith unto him, Verily I say unto thee, That this day, even in this night, before the cock crow twice, thou shalt deny me thrice." But the Lord's love for Peter never ceased.

Sometimes you might get aggravated with your colleagues, your children, or your spouse because they don't seem to be growing spiritually. Think for a moment of Jesus. He saw great potential in Peter, but He knew all along that Peter would deny Him! Commentator J. C. Ryle said, "Christ allowed the disciples to be His intimate friends and companions, knowing perfectly well what they would one day do. He granted them the mighty privilege of being continually with Him, and hearing His voice, with a clear foresight of the melancholy weakness and want of faith which they would exhibit at the end of His ministry."[4] Christ realized that this impetuous follower would become a great asset in establishing the church. The other disciples would need Peter to lead them.

God Doesn't Fit in a Box

Do you realize how important you are in the perfect plan of God? Although all of us sometimes feel like an afterthought in God's plan for the universe, it is essential that we realize that God loves us more than we could ever know. Yet sometimes the things He puts in our lives seem like an impenetrable wall we can't get through. It is at those times that we need to realize the truth of Isaiah 55:8-9: "For my thoughts are not your thoughts, neither are your ways my ways, saith the LORD. For as the heavens are higher than the earth, so are my ways higher than your ways, and my thoughts than your thoughts."

God is unlimited. There is nothing He can't do. Therefore what looks like a dead end from a temporary perspective really could be the beginning of a new time of growth. And yet many times we put God in a box. The box is our own conception of who He is. We want to tell Him what we want and how we want things done. In some ways, we almost want to take God's omnipotence and omniscience away from Him. Instead of realizing that we are an important part of the plan of God, we start thinking our plans are the most important.

We must unplug the desire for God's ways to suit our already made plans. Instead, we need to seek the Lord's direction before we make those plans. We tend to pray, "God, I really need that promotion," or, "I need a better car." Maybe we say, "If you'll just heal my sick child, I will praise you." We expect God to answer these prayers without realizing that His will may be for us to stay and learn something from that difficult boss. Or maybe he will bring a mechanic who fixes that car instead of giving you a new one. Perhaps your child continues to be sick, but a doctor or nurse is touched for Christ in the process. We sometimes tend to take God's answers as signs that God isn't listening to us and perhaps doesn't love us.

Yet if you understand that everything in your life is part of the perfect plan of God, then you will learn to trust the answers that He does give you. You will look back later and see that He always answers your prayers, but the answers are part of a much broader and more complete plan.

This isn't to say that God wants us to stay in a dead-end job, drive an old jalopy, or have a sick child. It is just that we should look at those things as part of the whole picture of God's will. The prayer you first prayed might be fulfilled in a different way than you initially thought. Yet in the answer you do receive, you will see that His plans are always best.[5]

Throughout Peter's life, the most important lesson he learned was that he was a part of God's plan. He needed to submit to it and trust God's provision. And it is important that we as believers realize that same principle.

Recently a dear friend and retired pastor, Joe Arnett, went to be with the Lord. For many years he rode the train down to the Pacific Garden Mission where he ministered to the men and women there. I always admired the great love and respect with which he treated the men in the mission. He submitted to God's wonderful provision throughout his life. Yet God's provision isn't always considered a "success" from a worldly perspective. And whether we admit it or not, we often use the world's definition of success as our own. Arnett didn't do that.

When Arnett's grandchildren would come to visit, he would stand at the door of his modest home and say, "Come on up to my mansion." His grandchildren knew what he meant. He was living for his home in heaven. What he had on earth didn't matter nearly as much as the heavenly treasure he was building every day.

I picture him now in heaven. He is living in a huge mansion, greater than anything he could have had here on earth. Someday he will say to his grandchildren, "Come on up to my mansion."

The world's definitions of success and failure are far from God's definitions. In spite of knowing this as Christians, sometimes we try to reconcile the worldly view of success with our prayers. Instead of being content to wait for God's provision, we want to hurry God up a bit. Don't try to force God into your timetable. Learn to challenge your own definition of success and bring it into line with Scripture.

Someone said, "Life makes sense backwards, but it must be lived forward." I can look back and see some of the things that caused heartbreak. But looking back I say, "God, I can see what You are doing now! This isn't the way I would have planned it, but I have found that it is the best way." I wish I had understood that principle at the beginning of my trials, but it seems that I had to go through the demanding times to appreciate what God was doing in my life.

Opposition is not necessarily a sign of God's disapproval. God sometimes allows the devil to thwart our progress, at least in the short run. Remember, the detours are what bring the greatest spiritual success.

Our church learned this lesson a few years ago when we went to get the permit for our current 76,000-square-foot auditorium and multipurpose addition. The church gathered to pray. With great fervor we asked God to give us the permit. But it was over two years before we received it and could start working on the building. It took a lot of time and aggravation—both of which we weren't counting on. (We rarely count on the fact that success on God's calendar might mean that our own time frame has to be adjusted!)

God's ways and thoughts were different from ours. And it was important that we as a church realized that. God did give us the victory, but it took a lot longer than we would have liked. God used the situation to make our church even stronger. Peter said later in one of his letters, "Beloved, think it not strange concerning the fiery trial which is to try you, as though some strange thing happened unto you: But rejoice, inasmuch as ye are partakers of Christ's sufferings; that, when his glory shall be revealed, ye may be glad also with exceeding joy" (1 Peter 4:12-13).

Does this mean the Christian has to show a hilarious happiness when he or she is facing trials? Hardships and difficulties are times for a deep joy that comes only from knowing that God is working all things through His will. It doesn't mean that you have to have a fake smile on your face. There is a depth to knowing God that can only be reached through hardship.

No Pain, No Gain

Sometimes the Lord's correction for our failures brings pain into our lives (Proverbs 3:12; Job 5:17). When the Lord steps in to help you use your failure as a stepping-stone to spiritual success, the solution isn't fun.

Think about the patient who visits the doctor for a painful throat. The doctor diagnoses a strep infection. But when the patient starts taking the prescribed medication, he doesn't feel immediate relief. We all know that the pain is only a symptom of a larger problem. The medicine will take a certain amount of time to work, and when it does work, it will eliminate the source of the problem, the infection.

If we have failed in some way by saying something in anger or letting a detour sidetrack us, it is easy to want an immediate fix. Just as the patient can be confident that the medicine is eliminating the problem, so you can be sure that God is still working through you.

The "easy life" of the Christian is a myth that should be put to rest. The detours of doubt, chuckholes of suffering, and highway patrolmen of hardship combine to develop our potential.

These troubles may not be what you envisioned for your life, but know that you can trust God's higher plan and His higher thoughts to bring you much farther than you could ever have brought yourself.

Pastor and author Charles Stanley wrote, "It has been said that where there is no pain, there is no gain. This phrase applies not only in the realm of athletics, but in the spiritual realm as well. The pattern we see in Christ's earthly ministry and in His personal pilgrimage bears this out. . . . Although suffering is usually the last thing to be considered useful, it is God's most useful tool. Nothing compares with suffering when it comes to bringing God glory, for nothing else highlights our dependence, weakness, and insecurity like suffering."[6]

See, life, when lived backwards, makes sense, but it must be lived forward. So instead of blaming God when bad things happen, practice praise. The bad things are all part of a potentially powerful plan of God.

Peter finally learned the meaning of spiritual success. It probably wasn't the kind of success he first visualized he would experience. There might be some who preach that everyone who is a Christian is promised wealth, that spiritual success brings riches as a sign of God's provision. I don't see that in the Bible. God isn't against wealth. Some of the most faithful men and women in the Bible had great riches. However, the basis for the success in these biblical characters was the moment-by-moment realization of God's faithfulness.

Watch Out! You're Standing on a Trap!

Susanne had worked for many years as a secretary. Day in and day out, she did all the tasks no one else wanted to do. Few even noticed. One day when taking her lunch break, one of Susanne's coworkers walked over to her desk and said, "Susanne, I've never told you this before, but you are indispensable to this company. Thanks for all the work you do."

Susanne was so surprised that the carton of milk she was holding fell to the floor. As she bent to clean up the mess, she couldn't help but think, *I finally get my first real compliment, and what do I do? I blow it. I'm so embarrassed.*

Doesn't it seem sometimes as if the moment something comes through that you've been waiting for, something else happens that negates the good thing? Susanne's embarrassment almost made her forget about the compliment she had received.

I think Peter might have felt this way in Mark 14. His devotion to the Lord was real. And he was willing to express that devotion. The trap of his pride was about to close. Jesus tried to say, "Watch out, Peter!" But Peter wasn't listening.

Let's look again at this passage in Mark. "And Jesus saith unto him, Verily I say unto thee, That this day, even in this night, before the cock crow twice, thou shalt deny me thrice. But he spake the more vehemently, If I should die with thee, I will not deny thee in any wise. Likewise also said they all" (Mark 14:30-31).

Peter's denial of the charge wasn't meant to be a contradiction of the Lord's words. He meant it in the best way. He felt his love for the Lord was strong, and he thought that even if all the disciples were offended, that despicable thing would never happen to him.

Peter said the wrong thing, but he said it in the right way. It wasn't wrong for Peter to defend Jesus. It was what he thought of himself that was wrong. Peter didn't realize how full of pride his statement was until later.

Peter had three problems. First, he elevated self above everything else. Second, he was boastful. Third, he contradicted the Word of God. Jesus said, "You will deny me," and Peter said, "I will not."

What is our own goodness really like? Do we really know ourselves? Obviously Peter didn't. Wrapped in pride, he made a rash and foolish vow.

Maybe you have experienced something similar in your own life. Perhaps you have taken on a new job before you prayed about God's will. Maybe you said something stupid that hurt a relationship. These things are easy to do because in the everyday moments, it is easy to forget we're not in charge. Looking at this example from Peter's life, we can learn not to be strong in the profession of our own strength. Strength only comes when we stand in our convictions, and those convictions only come from God.

All of us have a tendency to contradict the Word of God in our pride. I am reminded of this when in the midst of a discussion I start using the words *always* and *never* to my wife: "I never start arguments. I always take out the trash." When I say those two all-inclusive words, I am asking for trouble. Why? Because I don't know what I will do or say tomorrow. Only God knows. Therefore, I am speaking in pride when I say things like that. Instead of making statements I might not be able to back up, I try to say, "By the grace of God, I will never do that." This keeps my words in perspective and helps me to rely only on God's strength.

Peter never mentioned the strength of the Lord when he made the brash promise that he would never forsake the Lord. He should haven taken the Lord's admonition seriously. He had seen other prophecies the Lord had made come true. He should have realized that it was true he would deny the Lord even if he thought he never could.

Bursting the Balloon of Pride

Second Corinthians 10:5 offers the following help: "Casting down imaginations, and every high thing that exalteth itself against the knowledge of God, and bringing into captivity every thought to the obedience of Christ." This verse is the key to not saying the wrong thing. When we bring our thoughts and actions into captivity to Christ, we will find ourselves realizing daily that God's power is the only thing we can count on. We could never really know our own hearts.[7]

When the pastor preaches and says to beware of certain sins or problems, do you say, "No, not me, Lord! I'm not going to do that sin. I don't have to worry about that problem. That man in the pew behind me—he is the one who needs to worry about that. I don't think the preacher is speaking to me."

However, later that week or month you find yourself doing the very thing you said you wouldn't do. Every word of admonition that comes to us either from the Word of God or from a trusted godly friend should be heeded. Be aware of the sins you lean toward in your thought life and the statements that come out of your mouth that "exalt themselves" against the knowledge of God. The late A. W. Tozer, noted pastor and writer, stated that when the Christian realizes that it is God who needs to be exalted rather than himself, that is a chance to draw closer to God. "'Be thou exalted,'" he writes, "is the language of the victorious spiritual experience. It is a little key to unlock the door to great treasures of grace. . . . Let the seeking man reach a place where life and lips join to say continually, 'be thou exalted,' and a thousand minor problems will be solved at once. His Christian life ceases to be the complicated thing it had been before and becomes the very essence of simplicity."[8]

It is so important to keep your mind centered on Christ. Without His guidance, feelings of devotion can be bold. Yet feelings can't be trusted. Every thought needs to be in captivity to Christ. Only then will we be steady, mature believers.

It might be tempting to be hard on Peter, the statement he made, and his lack of follow-through. We shouldn't be though. If we were sitting at that last supper with Christ, and He made that particular statement to us, I'm sure there isn't a Christian who would have said, "Well, I know You know everything, Lord, so if You say I'm going to deny You, I will." I think all of us sitting there would have said the same thing Peter did. After all, the disciples had been with the Lord for three years and had faced hardship before. They had stayed true to Him so far; why would they leave now? They could never have grasped the magnitude of what Christ would experience. They could never have known their own terror on that dark night of the arrest. The crucible of Christ's sufferings would make them finally realize His greatness.

Success Equals Failure?

"Treasure in earthen vessels" is how 2 Corinthians 4:7 describes us. The Holy Spirit, the ever-constant guide of the Christian, is the treasure. He is the one who needs to shine. It is through the broken places of failure, anger, and disappointment that the treasure can shine. For it is not in our own strength that we serve. It is only in the realization that we are nothing and that He is everything that we can be a beacon to the world.

Throughout our study of Peter we will see that he didn't look at his mistakes in the same way we do. One man compared Peter to a rock you pick up at the beach. It might have all the color washed out of it and won't seem to have much worth. But if you break that rock open, you might find a beautiful interior full of purple amethysts and sparkling crystals. It is the same way with Christ. He takes our rough exteriors and splits them open to reveal beauty inside.

That angry statement, that failed business venture, that lack of patience with your children—all these times can be looked at as stepping-stones to spiritual success. I challenge you, dear friend, to realize your own weaknesses, just as Peter did.

Recognize with Peter that those times of failure "split" the rock, bringing him toward the path of spiritual maturity. This lesson is crucial to our understanding of the Christian life. Learn to split your own boulder of failure and disappointment. Inside you will find beauty beyond compare.

4

How to Cope in the Pressure Cooker

GROWING UP IN A SMALL SUBURB of Detroit, Jason and his younger sister Stephanie attended a Bible-believing church. As they got older, they became prominent members of the youth group. Then the youth pastor confessed to an affair with a woman in the church. Devastated, the young people stopped attending.

Marie's mother was a Christian, but she was also an alcoholic. She brought Marie up to fear God, and yet Marie dreaded the nights her mom stopped off for a couple of drinks after work. Her mother's problem was a great roadblock on Marie's spiritual journey.

Irene and Chad had two small children, Jill and Johnny. Grocery shopping, house cleaning, cooking—all these things had always been a challenge, but adding two small children to the mix made things almost unbearable. Then Johnny broke his leg playing baseball in the backyard. Irene didn't know if she could handle the added pressure of caring for him.

There is no question about it. Life is like a pressure cooker. The day-to-day problems never seem to end. As we continue to look at the drama of Christ's arrest and crucifixion, we will see how He handled the betrayal of one of His closest friends. Another close look will help us to avoid the deadly trap of greed. Finally we will focus on how Peter's unwillingness to wait for God's direction almost caused his own death. These reactions contain helpful keys to assist the believer during those times of pressure and trouble.

Betrayed, Forsaken—Yet Not Shaken

Sometimes another person's failure directly affects us. Consider the wronged partner in a marriage. Although he or she has been faithful, the marriage still ends in divorce. Or the person who loans money to a friend realizes he or she might never be paid back. The parent whose teenager rebels feels a deep sense of loss that can tear at the core of who he or she is.

In 1521 William Tyndale was one of the first persons to translate the New Testament into the English language. Since it was illegal at that time for people to read the Bible in any language other than Latin, his work put him in great danger. A man who pretended to be a friend but who was really an agent of the king later betrayed him.

A friend of mine experienced this kind of betrayal in his ministry. As a pastor, he was thrilled when Sam and June decided to get involved in church. Over time, the pastor and Sam became good friends. But ten years later the couple left the congregation. Sam refused to tell the pastor what was wrong.

Several years after that, a new family told the pastor that they didn't attend the church for many years because of some things they had heard about it. The pastor was surprised and hurt when he found out that Sam and June were the ones spreading the lies. I don't know if he will ever get over his sense of betrayal.

The events in the Garden of Gethsemane show Christ's great example of faithfulness in time of distress. The Lord reacted to abandonment and disloyalty with the human emotions we would all feel, but He also extended divine forgiveness.

Look at Matthew 26:46-50:

> *Rise, let us be going: behold, he is at hand that doth betray me. And while he yet spake, lo, Judas, one of the twelve, came, and with him a great multitude with swords and staves, from the chief priests and elders of the people. Now he that betrayed him gave them a sign, saying, Whomsoever I shall kiss, that same is he: hold him fast.*

> *And forthwith he came to Jesus, and said, Hail, master; and kissed him. And Jesus said unto him, Friend, wherefore art thou come? Then came they, and laid hands on Jesus, and took him.*

It was and still is a Middle Eastern custom to greet a friend with a kiss. Note that after Judas' greeting Jesus called him "friend." How could the Lord know his duplicity and still call him "friend"? The depth and love Christ has for every person is beyond our understanding! This unconditional love is certainly different from the way most people react to betrayal.

The Lord understood betrayal better than most of us ever could. For not only did He feel the pain of seeing Judas betray His trust, but because He was fully God, He knew from the first time He met this disciple the outcome of their friendship.

Jason and Stephanie were shocked at their youth pastor's indiscretion, but they had trusted him until they learned about the situation. Judas hurt the Lord on a deeper level. Imagine the Lord's pain during their every encounter! What must it have been like to live and work with someone for three years, knowing that person was planning the greatest backstabbing of all time?

We see both Christ's pain and His tenderness in the word *friend*. Christ was telling His disciple something very important by that term of affection. "Judas, I still love you. I know what you are doing. I have known this all along. Yet it is for this very sin that I am going to die. I am going to pay for all of your sins along with the sins of the world. I call you 'friend' because you are beloved. I hope you realize this before it's too late."

The Lord didn't excuse the sin of Judas. He had even predicted it. His unconditional forgiveness kept resentment and bitterness from blocking His love.

Looking at this example, it might be easy to say, "I can see why the Lord reacted that way, but after all, He was God. He had a perfect nature and couldn't have sinned. But I'm human. I couldn't possibly do the same." While it is true that there wasn't a trace of sin associated with our Savior, it is also true that He understood every human emotion that we experience. He was a man just as fully as He was God. Hebrews 4:15 says, "For we have not an high priest which cannot be touched with the feeling of our infirmities; but was in all points tempted like as we are, yet without sin."

Throughout the years, the people who have kept resentment and bitterness from ruining their lives relied on this divine love. The abandoned spouse can refuse to let her feelings of hate germinate by asking God to help her forgive. The hurt church member can realize that while people can let him down, God never will. Although it might be necessary to distance yourself from the person who hurt you, it is important that you learn to forgive.

Martin Luther, when summoned to the Diet of Worms and told to recant, said, "My conscience is held captive by the Word of God. Here I stand; I cannot do otherwise. God help me. Amen." I am sure Luther felt a sense of betrayal by the church, because he had faithfully served as a monk and teacher in the university for many years. Now the same church wanted him to recant, or they would kill him. Through the Lord's strength, Luther stood strong.

When you trusted Christ as your Savior, you became a partaker of the divine nature.[1] Therefore, when you are at the point that your strength is about to give out, that is the time for God's power to kick in. It is the time to pray this prayer: "Heavenly Father, I'm at the end of my strength. I have been hurt at the deepest level. I realize that I'm incapable of offering forgiveness on my own. So now I come asking for the grace I need to forgive." If you have done this, then know that you can have the victory to overcome even a friend's betrayal.

TIGHTFISTED TREACHERY

What drove Judas to do what he did? When the soldiers came to arrest Christ, the other disciples must have been shocked to see

Judas leading the way. After all, Judas had been with them day in and day out for three years. Judas had witnessed the miracles the Lord did. Judas had helped in the miraculous feeding of the 5,000. He had seen Christ raise people from the dead. To the superficial onlooker, Judas looked more "spiritual" than Peter. After all, Peter always said the wrong thing at the wrong time. Peter was presumptuous, unpolished, while Judas appeared poised, confident.

Judas didn't ask the prideful question about who would sit on either side of Christ in heaven, as James and John did.[2] When it came to spiritual matters, Peter was the first disciple to confess that he believed Christ was the Messiah.[3] Though he struggled, his faith was real. On the other hand, while Judas appeared to have it all together, his faith was a facade.

A guise of spirituality hid Judas' fatal flaw. A few days before the arrest of Christ, Jesus was eating dinner with Mary, Martha, and Lazarus. Mary, in a supreme act of devotion, broke a very expensive bottle of perfume and anointed the Lord's feet. She then wiped His feet with her hair. Her act of love was of great comfort to the Lord. At that moment Judas showed his true colors, saying in anger, "Why was not this ointment sold for three hundred pence, and given to the poor? This he said, not that he cared for the poor; but because he was a thief, and had the bag, and bare what was put therein. Then said Jesus, Let her alone: against the day of my burying hath she kept this. For the poor always ye have with you; but me ye have not always" (John 12:5–8).

Mary's gift was the fragrance of faithfulness while Judas' comment was the stench of stinginess. The whole situation could be described as "the perfume that caused a great stink." Note that Scripture says that Judas' declaration wasn't made because he loved the poor but because he was a thief and carried the group's money. Judas valued the perfume at 300 pence. In today's terms that would be a year's wages, anywhere from $25,000 to $30,000. Part of his anger was because he personally desired the money the ointment would bring. If Mary had not broken the box and used the contents, she might have given the alabaster box to Christ for His use. Judas might have been counting on Christ handing that same box to Judas and asking him to sell it. Judas could have taken his "cut," and he would have been rich. No question about it, Judas was an opportunist.

When he saw his chance at wealth being poured out, his thoughts could have been: *I've deprived myself for Him! I've slept out in the fields for Him! I've done everything, and I've received nothing in return.* This is a dangerous attitude, one that can trap all of us. Judas missed a vital truth. Who was the one who did only good for Judas? Who was the one who loved him unconditionally? Who brought the greatest happiness and friendship he ever experienced? The very one whom Judas said he served actually served him.

Jesus bypassed Judas' superficial spirituality, and God does the same for us. Believers aren't enrolled in a good works contest. Instead, the things we do are because of what He did for us. These acts of love have no price tag. Indeed, how could they? Jesus has already paid the ultimate price. Anything we do in return should come out of a thankful heart.

Dear friend, are you tempted to put a price tag on your works? When you teach that difficult Sunday school class, do you feel you should receive "extra points"? When you bring cookies to that crabby neighbor or sacrificially give money to the Lord's service, are you doing these things as acts of love? The Bible is clear that there will be rewards in heaven for the obedient believer, but these works do not help us gain entrance to that wonderful place. Stay away from an attitude of pride that like Judas says, "I have done so much for Christ," and instead say, "He has done so much for me. Why wouldn't I give my life for Him?"

WATCHING THE BOTTOM LINE

Judas' anger at the apparent waste made him blow his cover. Meeting with the scribes and elders, he agreed to lead them to the Lord. The agreed price was thirty pieces of silver, or about one-fourth of Mary's gift to Christ.[4] This could have been the amount Judas would have taken as his from the sale of Mary's ointment.

Judas' attitude, that life "owed" him, placed him in great danger. A man named Randolph felt the same way. He grew up in a home where money wasn't a problem. Whatever the latest collection craze, whatever toy everyone else had, his parents were happy to buy him. Then a bad investment forced his mom and dad to declare bankruptcy. Randolph found himself having to work his way through his last three years of college. Dropping out, he found a job at minimum wage. He deeply resented his poverty and found it easy to justify stealing from the company. He created false invoices, depositing the payments in a bank account with a phony name. He never stole very much—just enough so that he could maintain his lifestyle. One day he trusted Christ as his Savior. He realized it was time to confess his sin and pay his company back. After spending two years in jail, Randolph was determined to make a fresh start.

Judas saw his chance for riches slip through his hands, and so he let Christ slip through his hands. In turn, he let the thirty pieces of silver slip through his hands when he hung himself. Three years of being with Christ, and he ends up empty-handed. It was apparent that Judas was only interested in what Christ could do for him.

This is a great danger in our churches today. People sometimes attend church for all of the wrong reasons. They look at what they can get from the church, either from possible lucrative business deals or affirmation from others if they become a church leader. Then if those deals fail to materialize or no one appreciates their management, they get offended and withdraw from the fellowship.

These people should have been attending church from a different motivation. Our willingness to serve the Lord shouldn't come with preconceived ideas of how we can benefit. Our willingness should be just that, willingness.

When John D. Rockefeller went to church, people would try to sit by him. Instead of wanting to know him personally, they wanted him to share his wealth. When Rockefeller wasn't in town, church attendance was down.

Alexander the Great said of one of his soldiers, "He loves me because I'm Alexander; the people love me because I'm a king." Judas loved Jesus because He was a king. But he didn't love Him as Jesus.

WHAT HAVE YOU DONE FOR ME LATELY?

In looking at the difference between Mary's devotion and Judas' selfishness, I'd like to line myself up with Mary. Surely I make sacrifices for Christ based solely on showing my devotion. Yet I see myself with Judas' attitude more than I care to admit. All of us assume that Christ hasn't done enough for us lately. He gave us the greatest gift—eternal life. But instead of an attitude of thankfulness, we harbor greed.

Writer Eugene Petersen commented on this tendency:

> Among the apostles, the one absolutely stunning success was Judas, and the one thoroughly groveling failure was Peter. Judas was a success in the ways that most impress us: he was successful both financially and politically. He cleverly arranged to control the money of the apostolic band; he skillfully manipulated the political forces of the day. Peter on the other hand was impotent in a crisis and socially inept. At the arrest of Jesus, he collapsed . . . he was not the companion we would want with us in time of danger and he was not the kind of person we would feel comfortable with at a social occasion.

> Time, of course, has reversed our judgments on the two men. Judas is now a byword for betrayal, and Peter is one of the most honored names in the church, and in the world. Judas is a villain; Peter is a saint. Yet the world continues to chase after the successes of Judas, financial wealth and political power, and to defend itself against the failures of Peter.[5]

There are those who are continually burned by the world, and yet they persist in chasing after its illusive dreams. A woman named Sandy was trained from her early childhood to believe that the key to life was to get a good education. Sheltered in her growing up years by a loving Christian family, she was unprepared for campus life. When she met Samuel, she thought he was the man of her dreams. They lived together until they both graduated and then married. She had known Samuel wasn't a Christian, but the humanistic philosophy she was taught at school encouraged her to stop thinking so highly of her upbringing.

Marrying Samuel was the biggest mistake of her life. After years of hardship, the couple finally divorced, and Sandy struggled to put her life back together. She found a Bible-teaching church and enrolled her son in a private Christian school.

Now she faces a difficult decision. Sam, Jr., is nearing college age, and she struggles over what to tell him. She knows that he could be ruined by the influences he will encounter on campus, but she still wants him to get a degree so he can get a good job.

Her pastor has counseled Sam to enroll first in a Christian college so that his beliefs will be solid before he enters a secular school. Sam would be wise to listen to such counsel, and Sandy should listen to it too. Sandy should realize that if her belief system had been strong enough to start with, she would have avoided much heartache.

Many people are so enamored by the worldly system that when they are burned by it, they hardly notice. Like the baker who trains himself to take hot pans straight out of the oven, they don't notice the heat until their life is broken almost beyond repair. Fortunately Sandy broke the cycle with Sam, Jr. Her encouragement to solidify his own beliefs will save him years of hardship.

A Tale of Five Brooms

Judas can be compared to the man who opened a broom closet in a church to find five new brooms. He went to the one in charge of buying commodities and said, "Who authorized the buying of five brooms at once?"

The maintenance man couldn't give him an explanation that satisfied him. Then the man met with the pastor. The pastor tried to pacify him but finally in exasperation said, "Well, I don't know. Maybe we use a lot of brooms! Maybe there was a sale on brooms. But don't fall out of fellowship over it."

Some time later, over coffee with the church treasurer, the pastor told him about the broom situation. The treasurer smiled and said, "Pastor, I can understand why he was so upset."

The pastor said, "Would you please explain it to me."

The treasurer replied, "How would you feel if you saw everything you had given to the church in the past year tied up in five brooms?" That man was like Judas whose heart was tied up in accumulating riches on this earth.

Meet Mr. Sin

When agriculture students from U.S. and Canadian universities compete to identify problems in farm fields, it is like a World Series of Weeds. One year Iowa State took top honors in the Collegiate Weed Science Contest, which tests students' abilities to identify weeds, determine the right chemical to kill them, and diagnose herbicide failure.

"They need to be able to recognize weeds when they are tiny," said James Worthington of Western Kentucky University, president of the North Central Weed Science Society. "When they get big enough that anybody can recognize them, it's too late to do anything about them."

If it is important to learn to identify weeds when they are small, then what about identifying our own sinful tendencies before they get to be a big problem? The Bible says that every person has what I have termed a "Mr./Mrs. Sin" in his or her life. If this particular weakness is indulged in any way, it will grow to mammoth proportions. Some preachers call this a besetting sin. It is crucial that we learn to identify these sinful tendencies and avoid the situations where temptation is strong. Sin is not a piece of faulty software programmed into us as the result of bad environmental conditioning. It is hardwired into our human nature, embedded into us so deeply that nothing can totally eradicate it this side of heaven.

Sidney J. Harris, writer for the North American Syndicate, said, "Once we assuage our conscience by calling something a necessary evil, it begins to look more and more necessary and less and less evil."

Susannah Wesley defined this problem to her young son John: "Whatever weakens your reason, impairs the tenderness of your conscience, obscures your sense of God, and takes off the relish of spiritual things—that to you is sin."

No question about it, Judas' "Mr. Sin" was the love of money. First Timothy 6:10 explains, "For the love of money is the root of all evil: which while some coveted after, they have erred from the faith, and pierced themselves through with many sorrows."

The lion craves blood, the buzzards crave carrion; with every breath these creatures look for what they love the most. This was true of Judas and his love of money.

This worship of wealth defines many people's problem sin. They invest in every "get-rich-quick" scheme. They dream up ways to sell this or buy that to get rich. Someone else's besetting problem could be a tendency to place a greater emphasis on sports or shopping than they place on the Lord. Although these things aren't sin in and of themselves, done in excess they will take time that a person needs to spend with God.

Take a moment, dear friend, and identify the "Mr. or Mrs. Sin" in your life. Could it be you have a love of money and the things it can buy? Maybe it is an overemphasis on a hobby or an addiction you battled in the past. It could be a tendency to work so much you exclude your family, or maybe it is an inclination toward gossip. After you realize what it is, take definite steps to avoid its temptation. If this means changing your route home from work so you don't pass a liquor store, then do it. If it means staying away from people who gossip, then that might be what you need to do. If it means consciously placing your family above your job, then do that. Whatever you do, don't let "Mr. Sin" even get a foot in the door. He might knock, but you don't have to let him in!

Someone said, "Jesus can see the most tightly guarded and hidden areas of your heart, just as easily as you and I look through a window on a sunny day!" So open the windows wide and weed out that pesky family, "Mr. and Mrs. Sin"—before they get too big!

Earsplitting Earache

The odds of rolling a perfect game in bowling are about one in 225,000. A bowler collapsed when he qualified to join that brotherhood of 300. Another man just couldn't bring himself to play the final ball of an otherwise perfect game. Instead, he silently packed his shoes and ball and walked out—and never again set foot inside a bowling alley!

Pressure does different things to different people. Studying Peter's role in the arrest of Christ, we find an episode that is characteristic of what we have seen about him in the last chapter: "Then Simon Peter having a sword drew it, and smote the high priest's servant, and cut off his right ear. The servant's name was

Malchus. Then said Jesus unto Peter, Put up thy sword into the sheath: the cup which my Father hath given me, shall I not drink it?" (John 18:10-11).

Peter was ready to fight the entire temple guard. When he went for the servant's ear, he really meant to go for his head. Impetuous, impulsive Peter was always ready to do the job—just not in the way Christ would have him do it. He should have seen that the Lord wasn't resisting the arrest. He should have remembered the things Jesus had told him about His death. Peter's "Mr. Sin" was his reliance on his own strength. Think for a moment about the servant! That must have been one earache! It is a miracle that Peter wasn't carted off to be crucified with Christ after doing that deed.

When the Israelites stood at the Red Sea in Exodus 14:11-12, they were in as bad a situation as Christ and the disciples in the Garden of Gethsemane. Being pursued by the Egyptians, the children of Israel didn't know whether they should swim for it, turn and fight a hopeless battle, or just give up.

Have you ever experienced those feelings when you were at the brink of a difficult situation? It is at those times that you need to learn what Moses said: "Fear ye not, stand still, and see the salvation of the LORD, which he will show to you to day: for the Egyptians whom ye have seen to day, ye shall see them again no more for ever. The LORD shall fight for you, and ye shall hold your peace" (Exodus 14:13-14). It was time for the people to wait, and in their waiting they would show their trust in the Lord. Miraculously, the sea parted, allowing the people to cross on dry land.

Commentator J. C. Ryle said, "We fancy sometimes, like Peter, that there are some things we could not possibly do. We look pityingly upon others who fall, and plume ourselves in the thought that at any rate, we should not have done so. We know nothing at all. The seeds of every sin are latent in our hearts. Like Peter, we think we can do wonders for Christ, and like Peter, we learn by bitter experience that we have no might and power at all. A humble sense of our own innate weakness, a constant dependency on the Strong for strength, a daily prayer to be held up, because we cannot hold up ourselves—these are the true secrets of safety."[6]

Are you facing some situation that brings fear? Has an important job interview been scheduled? Is your marriage undergoing a crisis? Perhaps you are dating someone, and you aren't sure if you are ready for marriage. Is your child having a hard time making friends, but you can't really help him? Whatever you face, learn this lesson from Peter. Maybe you need to wait for God to show you His will. Once you have prayed and placed your burden in His hands, you can be assured that He will give you the wisdom you need. Don't jump ahead and cut off someone's ear! Someone has said, "One of the keys to the Christian life is to toil awhile, endure awhile, and believe awhile." In those times when life is the most difficult, maybe you need to step back, take a deep breath, and wait for God to work.

Strength in Times of Stress

If someone you trusted has hurt you, then studying how Christ reacted to Judas' betrayal and the disciples' abandonment will give you strength. If you have a problem in your life that is keeping you from serving the Lord fully, then looking at the life of Judas will help you prevent a particular sin from causing ruin. If you are like Peter—you tend to run ahead of God's plan and do the rash thing instead of waiting for guidance, then examining his tendencies will help you to wait for the go-ahead from God the next time you face a trial.

May you learn to pray for His strength to handle the difficult times. As you choose to follow His leading, you will experience victory and blessing even when you are in the pressure cooker of life!

5

How Could a Christian Do *That*?

WITH A CATLIKE MOVE, the thirteen-year-old stole the basketball from an opposing team member, dribbled down the court, and sank an easy shot. The crowd rose to its feet, clapping thunderously. The score was tied. Calling a time-out, Coach Jenkins gathered the excited boys around him and mapped out what he felt was a winning strategy on his clipboard.

As the clock started ticking down, Jenkins watched as his players perfectly executed his plan. Then a player took a moment too long to decide where to pass the ball. An opposing team member lunged for it. Panicking, the young man passed the ball to a player on the opposite team. The other player wasted no time. Turning and dribbling down the court, he swished in an easy shot just as the clock ran out. Jenkins threw down his clipboard in anger.

Jenkins's disappointment at the failed play mirrors the dissatisfaction a woman named Anita had with her job. Known for her attention to detail, she had come in her three-year stint with the company from the mailroom to lower management. Then a rumor went around the office that she was about to be promoted. One morning she met with her supervisor and found out someone else had received the coveted position. Anita had been strongly considered, but in her last report she had forgotten crucial details, and that omission had hindered the project's success. It took a long time for Anita to recover from her disappointment.

When we devote ourselves to an assignment, only to have our own error cause failure, it is hard to recover from the emotional devastation. Although we know of stories of those who failed many times before they became successful, it is sometimes hard to equate their experience with our own.

Comic strip creator Charles Schulz's drawings were turned down many times. First they were rejected by the editor of his high school yearbook and then by the editor at Walt Disney Studios, but his comic strip finally took off when he decided to reflect his own life of rejection in "Peanuts."[1]

In 1978 Bernie Marcus, the son of a poor Russian cabinet-maker in Newark, New Jersey, was fired from Handy Dan, a do-it-yourself hardware retailer. That prompted Marcus to team up with Arthur Blank to start a new business. In 1979 they opened their first store in Atlanta, Georgia. It was called The Home Depot. Today The Home Depot has more than 760 stores, and each year the corporation does more than $30 billion in sales.[2]

These stories are inspirational and encouraging. But when we are fired, we aren't prepared for the disappointment. When that surefire plan we suggested doesn't work, we don't always feel like digging in and trying harder. That motivational story is not always so motivating when we look at our own lives. Although we recognize that successful people sometimes fail, when *we* fail, it is hard not to feel alone.

Twenty-one-year-old Mohammed Ismail was arrested by the Egyptian police in October 1990. Two of his friends had been arrested eleven days earlier. The three former Moslems had trusted Christ as their Savior. They were tortured with electric shocks, beaten, and threatened with rape. At their trial they were declared innocent and released, but then they were arrested again. Under extreme persecution, the three converted again to the Muslim religion and were released.[3] It seems that the torture was too much for their faith.

It is hard to fault Ismail and his friends for denying their Lord. Many times believers do the same thing by not speaking up for Christ. They feel embarrassed when they try to share their beliefs.

How do we get past these feelings of failure? How do we recover when the failed marriage, the rebellious teenager, the disappointed boss is a result of our own mistakes? There is first the pain of the broken relationship, but even after that, the self-recrimination is beyond words.

Those dark moments make the future seem bleak and depressing. The moment the apostle Peter committed his greatest sin, there is probably no one who felt his future was darker. But his faithlessness in the face of the Lord's faithfulness drives home a powerful point. Peter's failure brought him on a spiritual journey toward wholeness and holiness. If you dare to follow that same journey, then you too will learn how to get past those times of disappointment and frustration at your own inadequacies.

The Torture Chamber of Self

As we progress through the events of the arrest and crucifixion of Jesus, we focus our attention on the main life-changing event in Peter's story, his denial of the Lord. If this had happened to a new believer, perhaps this sin would have been more understandable. After all, new faith is tender and fresh, not yet grounded in knowledge.

Peter wasn't a new believer. He had followed the Lord closely, completely. He had given three years of his life to the Lord's service. He had the best Bible education he could ever have had by the most knowledgeable, fascinating teacher of all, the Lord Jesus Christ. At the moment of Peter's third denial, he saw his life of studying, observing, loving, and learning as a disciple going down the drain.

Outwardly Peter had all the earmarks of a spiritual person. At the Last Supper Peter loudly vocalized his support and loyalty to Christ. At the Garden of Gethsemane, Peter rashly showed devotion by cutting off Malchus' ear. I have mentioned before that Peter was the first disciple to confess that Jesus was the Christ. All of these things seemed to add up to one spiritual person.

However, the flaw in Peter's life was inward. It was hidden, like a hideous tumor that insidiously wraps itself around vital organs of the body. Many times it isn't even the symptoms of the disease that drive the person to the doctor. Maybe a cold that won't go away or a slight irritating pain initiates a fifteen-minute visit. But in the examining room the truth is learned. The discomfort that first made the person seek help is but a small blip on the screen compared to the lethal disease within. Deep inside a cancer has been found that could eventually claim the life of its victim.

Peter didn't understand this deep cancer of the soul until he hotly denied the Lord and felt the sudden horrifying realization of his actions. His shame, discouragement, and overwhelming sense of humiliation brought him to the bottomless pit of disgrace.

Lurking in the Shadows

There must have been a slight chill to the deepening day as the soldiers led Jesus from the Garden of Gethsemane to His mock trial. Peter found himself wandering after the group far enough away so that no one would know him. Look at Mark 14:53-56: "And they led Jesus away to the high priest: and with him were assembled all the chief priests and the elders and the scribes. And Peter followed him afar off, even into the palace of the high priest: and he sat with the servants, and warmed himself at the fire. And the chief priests and all the council sought for witness against Jesus to put him to death; and found none. For many bare false witness against him, but their witness agreed not together."

The servants outside the palace of the high priest had started the fire. It probably wasn't very big, maybe just a few pieces of scrap wood that kept the flames burning. A few servants sat around it. Peter probably sank into the shadows, hoping the flickering firelight wouldn't light his face. He did not want to be recognized. His heart was in agony, and his emotions were in turmoil as he thought about what was going on in the judgment hall.

The city had been in an uproar for the past few days. The followers of Jesus were disappointed that apparently all their hopes were going to end. Peter knew that if Jesus were condemned, the Jewish leaders would want Him put to death before the Sabbath began. Since the Roman method was crucifixion, Peter had probably witnessed this type of death before. He knew there was a very real possibility that Christ would be crucified.

Commentator G. Campbell Morgan said, "He [Peter] could not see how suffering could be the way to the throne. He could not see how his Master's going to Jerusalem and being ill-treated, and finally—for he would use no other word—murdered, could issue in the building of that glorious Church to which his Lord had just made reference."[4] As Peter sat there, he might have pondered Christ's words, "Thou art Peter, and upon this rock I will build my church; and the gates of hell shall not prevail against it."[5]

There might be another reason Peter stayed far away. His own deed of cutting off Malchus' ear probably hadn't put him into favor with the Jewish leaders. That, coupled with the fact that they might arrest the followers of Jesus as well, made Peter very cautious.

I can understand Peter's desire to be incognito. There have been times in my life when I didn't want anyone to know who I was either. During my high school years, I attended Paducah Tillman High School in Paducah, Kentucky. This school was run like a tight ship with our principal, Mr. Munchler, at the helm. One day shortly after I arrived at school, I ran into a friend named Larry Riley in the hall.

"James Allen [when I was growing up, I was called by my full name], I don't feel like going to school today," he said. "Let's get out of here!"

It was a beautiful spring day, and it seemed like a great plan. Both of us were out the door in a flash. Traveling several blocks to where no one would know us, we entered a small grocery store, and Larry called a taxi. But when the taxi pulled up, we were surprised and dismayed to find one of the teachers from the school sitting in the backseat!

"Where are you boys going?" she asked.

I had to think fast. "To school," I said.

She seemed surprised that two healthy young men would ride a taxi to school just two blocks away. When we arrived, our hearts almost gave way again when we realized that Mr. Munchler saw us getting out of the taxi.

"Why did you boys ride a taxi to school?" he asked.

"We were late, and so we needed to catch a taxi," I explained.

You can imagine that Larry and I never ditched school again after that!

Just as Larry and I were found out, so one of the maids is about to ask Peter a question he will find pretty hard to answer.

Triple Trouble

> And as Peter was beneath in the palace, there cometh one of the maids of the high priest: And when she saw Peter warming himself, she looked upon him, and said, And thou also wast with Jesus of Nazareth. But he denied, saying, I know not, neither understand I what thou sayest. And he went out into the porch; and the cock crew. And a maid saw him again, and began to say to them that stood by, This is one of them. And he denied it again. And a little after, they that stood by said again to Peter, Surely thou art one of them: for thou art a Galilean, and thy speech agreeth thereto. But he began to curse and to swear, say-

> ing, I know not this man of whom ye speak. And the second time the cock crew. And Peter called to mind the word that Jesus said unto him, Before the cock crow twice, thou shalt deny me thrice. And when he thought thereon, he wept. (Mark 14:66-72)

Peter must have felt that the entire world was insistent on discovering his relationship to the Lord. First a young maid asks if he was with Jesus, and Peter says no. Probably the same girl sees him again and says to the crowd, "This is one of them." Peter angrily denies the charge. Peter stands out in that crowd the way a Texan would in Peoria, Illinois. His Galilean accent betrays him, and once again he is asked if he is a follower of Christ. Cursing and swearing, Peter says, "No, I don't even know Jesus!"

Then all Peter's senses combine in a terrible convergence of comprehension. First his hearing is indelibly stamped with a rooster's crowing. Then Luke 22:61 records that just as Peter denies the Lord the third time, the Lord turns and looks upon Peter. This isn't a piercing look of anger. This is a loving look—a look to say, "Even though I predicted that you would do this, Peter, and even though you have denied Me in My moment of deepest need, I love you beyond comprehension." Therefore, both Peter's ears and his eyes unite the evidence of what he has just done. Add to that the acrid smell of the fire and the taste of his salty tears as he goes out and weeps bitterly.

Pastor and writer M. R. DeHaan said, "Right then and there Peter lost his joy and fellowship with the Lord. He was not cast out, nor did he cease to be a child of God, but he lost the victory of discipleship."[6] Peter probably thought his Christian life was over then, but the reality was that it was just beginning. The best thing Peter could have done at the moment was get as close as he could to the Lord. However, he did the next best thing: He went off by himself so he could weep himself dry. Peter glimpsed now the depth of wickedness in his own soul. The ugly tumor of pride revealed itself long enough for him to suffer revulsion and shock.

The glimpse that Peter caught of himself changed his life. Never again did he say the brash things he used to say. Never again did he overestimate his own importance. Never again did he allow pride free rein.

The anguished wife has this same kind of moment when she realizes she was to blame for a failed marriage. The college student who is caught for cheating on a big exam anguishes when he realizes he won't be able to clear his record. The person who hurt a close friend while under the influence of alcohol suffers this kind of remorse once he comes back to himself.

An early church writer said that Peter never again heard the common sound of the rooster's crowing without remembering his terrible deed. However, when his tears flowed, he was also reminded of God's grace. When he heard a rooster crow, along with the memory of his own sin came the memory of God's mercy and forgiveness. He didn't let that sound get him down. Instead, he used it as a time to remember the Lord's compassion.

Are there certain memories that you would rather forget? Maybe something tangible reminds you of a past event in your life. These physical reminders can bring unbearable guilt. It is essential that, like Peter, you remember both your sin and the grace that has covered that sin. God helped you through that time, possibly keeping you from suffering more. Learn as Peter did to use your memories for good and not for evil. Don't let them torment you. Instead, use them as a time to remember the loving forgiveness of your great God.

THE WAY HOME

Peter's tears of torment eventually brought deep healing. It is said that tough men don't cry. Yet Peter was one of the toughest of the tough men, and it was not until he cried bitter tears that he experienced growth and maturity in his Christian life.

A father was dropping off his little girl at Sunday school and was surprised when he glimpsed a tear in her eye. "Why are you crying, honey?" he asked.

"Because I know after you drop me off, you will go and drink until you are drunk, and you will come home and be mean to Mommy," she replied.

The man was hurt to the quick. He realized he was hurting his entire family by his drinking, which to him had been no big deal. He wept bitter tears that day, and after that Sunday he began going to church. His remorse was the catalyst for change.

Peter's tears eventually drove him to Jesus' side. He was one of the first disciples to enter Jesus' tomb and discover only grave clothes: "Then arose Peter, and ran unto the sepulchre; and stooping down, he beheld the linen clothes laid by themselves, and departed, wondering in himself at that which was come to pass."[7]

He realized that Jesus' payment on the cross for the sins of the world included his own terrible sin of denying the Savior. In the same way, when the time of remorse comes, be sure you go first to the Lord Jesus. The great early American preacher Jonathan Edwards said, "How happy you would be if your hearts were but persuaded to close with Jesus Christ! Then you would be out of all danger: whatever storms and tempests were without, you might rest securely within: you might hear the rushing of the wind, and the thunder roar abroad, while you are safe in this hiding-place."[8]

Judas had quite a different reaction than Peter to the realization of his sin. Judas returned his thirty pieces of silver to the high priest and said, "I have sinned in that I have betrayed the innocent blood. And they said, What is that to us? see thou to that. And he cast down the pieces of silver in the temple, and departed, and went and hanged himself" (Matthew 27:4-5).

Judas realized what his terrible deed had done, but because he had never accepted Christ as his Messiah, he had no one to turn to. If he had gone out and wept bitterly, as Peter had, he might have realized that Jesus still loved him despite his horrible sin. He would have had time to recall Christ's compassion even when he led the chief priests and elders to arrest Christ. He might have remembered Jesus' greeting of "friend." He would have recalled the Passover Supper and Jesus' knowledge that he was going to do this. He might have realized that Jesus was also dying on the cross for his own sin. As it was, he gave himself no time for reflection but immediately hung himself.

Peter's tears made him reflect finally on the love of Christ. Although Peter realized that he didn't deserve that love, he understood that Christ's love wasn't dependent on his merit anyway. This was precious knowledge indeed and helped Peter through the following dark days. Peter realized that his own love for the Lord was nothing unless it rested on the sure foundation of Christ's love.

Reflection is always a helpful tool for the Christian. If you have committed some terrible deed, don't be afraid to reflect on it. Just realize as you do that although Peter did one of the most awful deeds in the history of the world, the love Christ had for him never ceased. And so He has never stopped loving you. Not for one instant has He taken His eye off you. Perhaps you would like to pray the following prayer: "Lord, I have sinned. In studying Peter, I realize that if You could love him that much and could forgive him of his sin, then surely You have forgiven me. I rest in that forgiveness and thank You for granting it to me."

Steps for Spiritual Success

What did Peter do to turn his failure into a springboard for spiritual success? There were some definite steps that Peter took in order to move on in his walk with Christ. As I mentioned before, at the moment he denied the Lord, he probably thought his life as a disciple was at an end. In reality he was just beginning. Here are four of the principles Peter learned. If you study them and apply them to your life, they will give you the support and strength you need to overcome the frustration that accompanies failure.

Spiritual Success Step 1—Diagnose the Disease

Peter first learned to diagnose the disease. He looked at both the fact of his sin (denying the Lord three times) and the root of his sin (pride). He learned that if he nipped pride in the bud in the future, he would be less likely to commit greater sins.

My father was a Methodist preacher when I was growing up. He used to tell a story about a man in his church who prided himself on the fact that he could not accept a compliment. My dad once said to him, "I want to compliment you on the fact that you can't accept a compliment." The man said, "Thank you." When a person is full of pride, he is usually unaware of it until the Lord wakes him up.

Isaiah 2:12 states, "For the day of the LORD of hosts shall be upon every one that is proud and lofty, and upon every one that is lifted up; and he shall be brought low." First Corinthians 10:12 says, "Wherefore let him that thinketh he standeth take heed lest he fall."

Peter thought the chain of his spirituality was strong, but he missed a vital link. Once he was able to diagnose the problem, he was a changed man. When a huge tree stands in the forest, it might look strong—until it falls and all can see that the inside had rotted away. The decay from deep within finally caused the tree to fall. Peter learned to deal with the rotten core of pride in his life before it ruined him.

Realize too that God allowed these things to happen in Peter's life to make him a stronger person. I have found that the really tough times in my own life have brought out an appreciation and love for others that wasn't there before. Those hard times made me realize that He cares about me and that I need to lean on His strength rather than my own.

So if you have failed and you want to experience spiritual success, then learn the first thing Peter did to make a difference. Correctly diagnose the problem. Then treat that problem as your "Mr. Sin," as we talked about in the last chapter. Stay away from places, literature, etc., that would feed that part of your nature.

Spiritual Success Step 2—Study the Word of God

One spring a family drove from Fort Lauderdale to Tampa, Florida. As far as the eye could see, orange trees were loaded with fruit. When they stopped for breakfast, the dad ordered orange juice with his eggs.

"I'm sorry," the waitress said. "I can't bring you orange juice. Our machine is broken."

At first this man was dumbfounded. They were surrounded by millions of oranges, and he knew they had oranges in the kitchen—orange slices garnished the plates. What was the problem? No juice? Hardly. They were surrounded by thousands of gallons of juice. The problem was they had become dependent on a machine to get it.

Christians are sometimes like that. They may be surrounded by Bibles in their homes, but they have no nourishment for their souls. The problem is not a lack of spiritual food, but that many Christians haven't grown enough to know how to get it for themselves.[9]

Constant study of the Word of God will bring spiritual success. Every day a new insight can strengthen your faith. This is something that Peter learned after his failure. He needed to meditate on the words of the Lord Jesus Christ. He did this so much that eventually the Holy Spirit prompted him to write two books of the Bible.

If you want to learn this principle for success, then never miss a chance to receive spiritual nourishment. Going back to my Bible college days, I remember that at times it was easy to go out and sleep in my car during chapel services. I was exhausted from working two jobs, going to school, and trying to be a good husband and father. I justified my absence because no one really knew if I attended or not. Then one day one of my teachers brought a simple truth home. He said, "The one chapel service you miss could contain a message from God's Word that could have changed your life." I never missed chapel or any chance for spiritual growth after that.

When we come to His Word with sincere devotion and a willingness to obey, God will show us our hearts as we have never seen them before and will warn us about what may happen if we don't follow His will.[10]

Study your Bible, attend church and special services, talk of your faith—all these things will strengthen your resolve and help you to overcome failure, as they helped Peter.

Spiritual Success Step 3—Trust God Even When the Way Is Dark

When Peter sat by that small fire warming his hands, with his heart in turmoil, he should have remembered that the Lord had predicted the exact events taking place. As it was, instead of meditating on the Lord's words, his own faith was shaken to the core. When he denied the Lord, he realized he should have continued to trust the Lord, even though there was no apparent reason for doing so at the time.

This is probably the hardest lesson for the Christian to learn. For God does not work according to our rules or our time schedule. As we have discussed before, His thoughts and ways are above our own. So hang on the tightest when the night is the darkest. You will be tempted to let go. Whatever you do, don't lose faith. It is at those moments that God's glory will have the greatest chance to shine.

George Mueller said, "Faith does not operate in the realm of the possible. There is no glory for God in that which is humanly possible. Faith begins where man's power ends."

In 1996 a Chicago firefighter named Bill Heenan was teetering on a ladder when he made a one-arm catch of a screaming eight-year-old girl who hurled herself out of a sixth-floor window. This firefighter is quite a hero because in February of 2000, he was the first rescuer to reach his neighbors, an elderly couple trapped under charred rafters and bricks after a natural gas explosion. Recently this firefighter was critically injured while battling a blaze that gutted a home in the heart of the city.[11]

The eight-year-old girl showed faith in that firefighter when she jumped into his arm from the sixth floor. If she had stayed in the building, she would have burned to death. The little girl's choice to trust Heenan showed a faith fueled by necessity. In the Christian life, that is the most difficult kind of faith to have. When the flames of life are licking at your heels, it is tempting to check out another resource and lean on your own solutions. But it is at those times of desperation that we need to jump into the arms that are stronger than life itself. Even when the way is dark and questions remain, we need to make a conscious decision to trust His mighty strength.

Spiritual Success Step 4—Watch and Pray

Peter was warned repeatedly that the events of the arrest and trial would be difficult, but he didn't heed. Sometimes when you are in a trial, you can look back and see hints of God's preparation. Learn to heed advice from fellow Christians and prepare. As Jesus said, "Watch and pray that you enter not into temptation." Jesus was aware that the spirit might be willing, but our physical bodies are weak.

In Pass Christian, Mississippi, in 1969 a group of people were preparing to have a "hurricane party" in the face of a storm named

Camille. Their living quarters faced the beach, less than 250 feet from the surf. The wind was howling outside the Richelieu Apartments when Police Chief Jerry Peralta pulled up after dark. A man with a drink in his hand came out to the second-floor balcony and waved. The officer yelled, "You all need to clear out of here as quickly as you can. The storm is getting worse."

Another person joined the man on the balcony, and they laughed at Peralta's order. "This is my land," one of them yelled. "If you want me off, you'll have to arrest me."

Peralta didn't arrest anyone, but he wasn't able to persuade them to leave either. At 10:15 in the evening, the front wall of the storm came ashore. Scientists clocked Camille's wind speed at more than 205 miles per hour.

News reports later showed that the worst damage came at the little settlement in Pass Christian where twenty people were killed. Nothing was left of that three-story apartment building but the foundation. The only survivor was a five-year-old boy clinging to a mattress.[12]

Just as Officer Peralta's warnings went unheeded, so were Christ's warnings.[13] Peter, James, and John weren't ready for the difficulty of the trial. The simplest way they could have prepared was to get extra rest. Then when Jesus asked them to watch and pray, they could have done it without falling asleep. Their need for sleep was so great that Christ woke them three times, each time asking them to stay alert. But they found it impossible to stay awake. If they had prepared ahead of time, maybe they could have been a comfort to Christ in His last hours.

Sometimes when trials come, there isn't much warning. At those times we have to cope moment by moment, relying on the strength of God. But sometimes there are hints that something is going wrong. Those hints need to be taken seriously. Realize too that the Lord Himself must have prepared ahead of time by getting sufficient rest, for He was able to stay awake and pray.

Adequate nutrition and rest go a long way toward making us better able to cope in times of crisis. When that loved one is sick or the family is in a financial crisis, sometimes just getting enough rest will help the situation to resolve more quickly. We also need to spend extra time in the Word of God and in prayer. These sessions will prepare us for situations when we might not have time to study. This groundwork will give us the wisdom to face the trial.

So take a moment, friend, if you are facing a difficult time and tend to the needs of your body. You will be better equipped and be in a restful frame of mind. You will be able to see God's hand of guidance if you have prepared yourself spiritually, mentally, and physically. Peter learned this lesson the hard way.

THE FINAL LAP

When we identify those things that are problematic to our spiritual growth, we learn that even our best efforts will not change them. Then it is to the Lord's arms we must fly. If Peter had determined that on his own he would alter his ways, he could never have really changed. The Lord's mercy caught him up, transformed him, and set him on a rock. This mercy brought healing to the deepest part of his soul.

Since he had already trusted Christ as his Savior, he didn't do this in order to go to heaven. The Lord paid the penalty for all of Peter's sins, even his denial, when He hung on the cross. But the fellowship that Peter had so enjoyed with the Lord over the past three years needed to be restored. He needed to confess the sin of denial. But deeper than that, he needed to confess his own pride before he could enjoy again that sweet companionship with the Lord. Peter understood the words of the psalmist, "Create in me a clean heart, O God; and renew a right spirit within me." Peter's confession brought renewal, new life, and restoration to His walk with Christ.

Are you in need of this mercy? As it was freely offered to Peter, so it is offered to you. It is up to you to accept it. You can stubbornly hold on to your own strength, or you can accept His towering strength. You can clutch the tattered garments of your own pride, or you can wear the flowing forgiveness of grace. You can cling to your arrogance or clutch His gentleness. You can exchange your tears of embarrassment for His tears of love. So set your mind to confession, your heart toward His forgiveness, your soul to study, and let the overflowing river of God's pardon flood your entire being with newness of life.

6

Hope Even When It's Hopeless

RICK'S LIFETIME DREAM was to own a business. Saving every penny he could, he managed to start a landscaping company. The first few years went well. Rick put every dollar of profit he made right back into the company. But bad weather and a host of other problems eventually took their toll. Now Rick is barely scraping by. He wonders if it is worth it to continue.

Having grown up in a dysfunctional home, Teresa has had to overcome many difficulties. The most challenging is that she is hearing-impaired. She is married, with three small children. Recently her mother was diagnosed with cancer. Teresa now wonders why she has to face this new difficulty when she has had to overcome so much in the past.

Sometimes no matter how much effort you give, the return seems minimal at best. All your dreams of owning a booming business, being a model son or daughter, or perhaps even becoming a millionaire remain simply that—dreams. Maybe you conquered many daunting problems in order to receive a certain position at work, only to find yet another hardship crouching at your door. Our human tendency is to want to quit. We try to block out the harsh realities of life by pulling the covers over our heads.

Rick and Teresa are reacting to the latest obstacles in their lives the same way we do. They feel that because in the past they have overcome great odds, somehow it should be easier now. Life shouldn't continue to dish out hardship because somehow they deserve better treatment.

Yet this mind-set is directly opposite to the one that God has set forth in His Word. The idea that we deserve special treatment is a worldly one. The world says, "Give me the easy road because I deserve it," while God says, "The road for the Christian is hard, but those times of trial will make you into the person I want you to be."

It is sometimes challenging to embrace this concept in a practical way when adversity comes. It is easy to say to a pastor or a trusted Christian friend, "I am going through a difficult time, but I know God will take care of me." However, actually living as if we believe God will take care of us is much harder to do.

FAILURE IS NORMAL BUT NOT PERMANENT

Peter suffered from this same dilemma. He knew theologically that Jesus was the Messiah, but living this out on the night of the arrest and crucifixion was much more demanding. Though he had experienced some hardship while following Christ, most of those times didn't affect him personally. Jesus Christ suffered attacks from the moment He began His ministry. Peter's role in the three years he followed Christ was to listen and learn. He might have thought he understood what the Christian life was really like until he personally faced hardship.

We all long for what we call a "normal" existence. We want the business to run okay, the children to behave, and our relationships to stay intact. Occasionally the jagged pieces of our lives do fall into place. Maybe one day you got up on time, ate an unhurried breakfast with the children, serenely dropped them off at school, had a productive day at work, and then returned home with plenty of time to prepare dinner. This might happen once or twice a year, but we take a mental snapshot of that day and label it "normal."

When things fall out of place (which they do every other day!), we compare the current situation to our mental image. When the two pictures don't line up, we get discouraged. Instead of working to find a solution, we wish things would go back to "normal," even though normal wasn't realistic in the first place.

We live in a fairy-tale society. Billboards show beautiful people who are the perceived right weight. The men are always macho bodybuilder types who by their very presence seem to say that if you drink beer, smoke cigarettes, or use whatever else they are advertising, then you will be as handsome and happy as they are. The problem is that if you asked most "beautiful" people what they really thought of themselves, you would probably hear a host of disparaging comments about their own appearance. Those same people are putting themselves up against an impossible standard of beauty—one that rests solely on physical appearance. And yet we continue to think that this standard is "normal" and therefore desirable.

Think about the New Year when people make resolutions to change certain behaviors. Maybe someone decides to go to the doctor for a physical or lose some weight. Others may determine to take up a certain exercise program or go to church more often. If the person can somehow equate this habit as a "normal" part of life, then the new habit will become routine. The problem is that when we start to carry out these new resolutions, we perceive the discipline as unusual. We feel deprived every time we choose to eat less or get up early to exercise. The changes don't last.

We all know that life isn't very normal, and neither is the believer's life. This inability to accept the Christian life as it really is can affect our ability to use hardship as a time of spiritual growth. If we perceive suffering as normal, then we won't continually be looking for a way out of the situation. God can then use the difficulty to mold and shape us into His image. We will recognize then that even failure is normal. Instead of longing for life to return to an easier time, we will learn to grow and mature in the midst of the distress.

When Peter heard the rooster crow twice, he might have thought, *I don't know why I keep trying! I am a despicable failure.*

Peter finally began to understand that suffering, hardship, and failure were a normal part of life. He learned from his failure at the cross that Christ's hope was always there in spite of the hopelessness of his sin.

A preacher might feel like quitting when he gives of himself day after day to his church, only to find that his own board wants him to resign. The woman who gives everything for the sake of a relationship feels this way when she finds out that she was wasting her time. Against other people's advice, a man might bring a partner into his business and then find out his partner is corrupt. He feels like giving up because of his mistake.

There is a quality in Peter's life that can inspire all of us. Peter found out that failure, though normal, was not permanent. Although he felt devastated at the terrible sin he had committed, he learned that admitting his mistakes were part of growing toward a deeper faith and commitment in his walk with Christ. In his weakness, he found the strength from a higher and greater Source. His own strength was a chasm of inadequacy. He discovered instead a never-ending well of strength and hope in the love of Christ.

How to Obtain Hope

Peter shares many practical principles for overcoming trials in his first letter. These tips can help the man or woman who is finding the Christian life less appealing because of the hard times. Peter learned to persist in spite of his life being stuck in the "abnormal" mode, and so can you. His first principle might seem simple at first, but on it hinges the secret of enduring hardship. Look at 1 Peter 1:3: "Blessed be the God and Father of our Lord Jesus Christ, which according to his abundant mercy hath begotten us again unto a lively hope by the resurrection of Jesus Christ from the dead."

This verse mentions a "lively" hope. The word *lively* is used in contrast to the vague, shadowed, and uncertain kind of hope most people have.[1] This lively hope points in a direction quite different from the path we have trodden in the past that was littered with false expectations.

Before Peter met Jesus, he was a fisherman. He didn't fish for recreation. He fished for a living. When he began to follow Jesus, he saw that his dream to be a successful fisherman was a false hope compared to the hope he found in Christ.

When I was growing up, my goal was to be a politician. My intent when I entered the University of Kentucky was to graduate and go into politics. But along the way, I realized that God could bring me a hope and a reason for living far beyond what I had dreamed for myself.

While attending the university, I received a call from the district superintendent of the Methodist Church. Since my father was a Methodist preacher, this man offered me the pastorate of a small church. I was surprised they wanted a young college student who wasn't exactly living a godly life to do this. He felt though that I was the man for the job. The church was only forty miles from the university, and the district superintendent told me I could live in the parsonage. I knew this would help me with my college expenses.

The more I thought about it, the better the offer sounded. The first Sunday I learned that the dean of men from the university was a former pastor of the church. So much for doing this job incognito!

I gained popularity because my exhortations were brief and to the point (I read the sermon from a book). Because of my short sermons, the congregation dined at the local restaurants after church before the Baptists let out. Everything was going along pretty smoothly. I continued to attend the university, and I enjoyed living in the parsonage and making some extra money.

Then I met a wonderful Christian couple, Jo and Bill Norris. When she invited me into their home, I had the honor of praying with her and Bill. I hadn't prayed too often in my life except when I was in trouble, so praying with Jo and her husband was quite an experience. Their prayers were fervent and heartfelt, almost as if heaven came down for a moment and touched the earth.

One day she said, "James, I think after you are done with school, you are going to be a preacher."

I said, "Jo, you don't know what you are talking about! I want to go into politics."

One day a few friends shared with me something I had never heard before—the clear, simple gospel message. I had been raised believing that if you did enough good deeds, you would make it into heaven. Opening the Bible, they showed me a verse I had never read before: "For by grace are ye saved through faith; and that not of yourselves: it is the gift of God: Not of works, lest any man should boast" (Ephesians 2:8-9).

What a surprise to learn that salvation wasn't dependent on what I did, but rather on Christ's work on the cross! That day I placed my trust in Jesus Christ. For the first time I knew I was going to heaven, not on my own merit, but on His. God was beginning to reveal His plan for my life. I had taken the first step by trusting Christ as my Savior. Jo continued to tell me that she was praying I would go into the ministry.

A Call to Preach

One Sunday afternoon I rested in the parsonage alone. I felt strangely led to drive down a road I'd never been on before. I stopped at a place where the creek ran over the road. There was no bridge, and the water was too deep to drive through. I waded across to the other side. Getting back on dry land, I walked about 100 feet and suddenly heard an African-American man praying on his knees. Not knowing what to do, I tried to keep quiet so I wouldn't disturb him.

Then he looked up. I couldn't help but notice his eyes. They seemed to look into my very soul. Then his earthshaking statement brought instant tears to my eyes. He said, "Are you the preacher I've been praying for?"

For a moment it was as if the Lord had stopped the globe. The call couldn't have been more clear. I was to be one of God's preachers.

I looked out on the little hills that surrounded the creek. I imagined three crosses standing tall and ugly against the setting sun. And I knew I would gladly spend my life telling others how the cross could transform their lives just as it had mine.

I prayed, "Lord, I'm not much, but what I am, I give to you." At that moment I surrendered to the call of God. Just as Peter cast down his nets and followed Jesus, I realized that whatever God wanted me to do, I would do it. My dreams of doing something else now seemed empty. This new direction flooded my life with hope.

Some people have said that I have sacrificed to serve the Lord. And yet through the years one truth has remained startlingly clear. I have surrendered nothing. As Paul said, he counted his former life as dung when he recognized the higher calling of God (Philippians 3:8). Many times in the years since, I have felt like throwing in the towel. But when I come to that point, I go back to those imaginary crosses and that dear man who was praying for me. I find then that I can't give up. Jesus has given too much to me for me to quit.

Thanks to that day, I have experienced great joy in my life. Linda has been a dear companion throughout the entire journey. Both of my children have married Christian spouses, and they all joyfully serve the Lord. My grandchildren are a continual delight. I have a church where people are being transformed into the image of Christ, and that knowledge brings me untold joy. I can say that not only *will* it be worth it all—it *has* been worth it all!

Feeding on False Hope

My dream of entering politics was based on presumption rather than reality. This new hope was real, dynamic, courageous, and patient. This hope activated and motivated me. I realized that God had a purpose for me, and I could trust Him to fulfill that purpose in my life.[2] Writer Warren Wiersbe said, "A 'living hope' is one that has life in it. And therefore can give life to us. Because it has life, it grows and becomes greater and more beautiful as time goes on. Time destroys most hopes; they fade and then die. But the passing of time only makes a Christian's hope that much more glorious."[3]

A woman named Isobel found this hope just after the birth of her first child. Before she became pregnant, she sometimes hated life. Although outwardly she was carefree, inwardly she was miserable. But when she held her new baby in her arms, she realized he was a gift from God. Scriptures she had memorized as a child came back to her. The God she thought had forgotten still cared about her. A stirring of something she could only call hope moved within her. For the first time, she realized there *is* something to live for. When Isobel thinks of hope, she thinks of her baby, and then she thinks of God's faithfulness.

People are searching for this hope. Their quest sometimes leads them to the counterfeit. A chilling example of this occurred when thirty-nine members of the cult known as Heaven's Gate took their own lives. Authorities discovered videotapes in which the leader of the cult described their hoped-for space encounters. Members came before the camera two at a time, side by side, to say their last good-byes. One woman said, "Maybe they are crazy for all I know, but I don't have any choice but to go for it, because I've been on this planet for thirty-one years, and there's nothing here for me."[4]

This is hope based on wishful thinking—a false dream of a

UFO rescue. Other individuals think that if they just could earn enough money, then hope will come bundled in the package of material blessings.

A family once spent some time at a luxurious resort. While they were on the elevator, an obviously wealthy woman stepped on, carrying some heavy groceries. The man commented that she must be getting her exercise for the day. She responded, "Sure, I'm doing my daily exercise. But what difference does it make how much exercise I'm getting? I'm still getting older, and from here on out it's downhill to the inevitable!" This woman possessed many assets our culture considers important, but she lacked life's most valuable treasure—hope for her future.

A preacher writes, "The greatest need of almost everyone I know, including myself, is the need for hope."[5]

When Christ rose from the dead, Peter and the disciples realized that everything He had said was true. This event poured courage into their faltering hearts. The sermons they preached after this event were inspiring and bold, because they realized that their hope was vibrant and vital.

A biblical view of hope is the joyful expectation of good. Christian hope is *certainty*. One writer said, "Hope is not the prospect of what might happen but the prospect of what is already guaranteed."

Peter wrote his first epistle just before the greatest wave of persecution the church had experienced yet. Nero was in power. He blamed a terrible fire that occurred in Rome in A.D. 64 on the Christians. He was never able to make that charge stick, but he did succeed in convincing the people that believers were enemies of society. The intense persecution began. Tacitus, one of the early Roman historians, said that most of the Christians in Rome lost their lives during this time. From A.D. 63-68 believers by the thousands died in that city. They met in the catacombs because they were not able to meet openly. The name of Christ wasn't allowed to be spoken. In the next decade the persecution was carried on by Domitian out to the limits of the Roman Empire, and then it was continued by Trajan. The apostle Peter was martyred during the first stage of persecution, as was the apostle Paul.

Peter wrote his epistle to believers in Asia Minor to warn them of the coming persecution. In the midst of this terrible ordeal, the Christians were reminded of their living hope. This hope was not based on false dreams. It was not based on a dead religion. It was based on a risen, living Savior.

When the Future Looks Bleak

This hope is critical for the person who is suffering and may see only more pain and worry ahead. The Christians who received this letter from Peter had only suffering to look forward to. The persecution wouldn't let up in their lifetimes or even in their children's lifetimes. But they were told to hold to their living hope.

During the Thirty Years War in the seventeenth century, German pastor Paul Gerhardt and his family were forced to flee their home. One night as they stayed in a small village inn, they felt destitute and afraid. Gerhardt's wife broke down and cried openly in despair. To comfort her, Gerhardt reminded her of Scripture promises about God's provision and keeping. Then, going out to the garden to be alone, he broke down and wept. He felt he had come to his darkest hour.

Sometimes after we are able to give someone else hope, we feel that we have let go of our own. When that happens, it is important to do what Gerhardt did. Go and get by yourself with the open Scriptures. Read, pray, cry if you need to—you *will* receive fresh hope from God.

Gerhardt felt the burden lift and sensed anew the Lord's presence. Taking his pen, he wrote a hymn that has brought comfort to many.

Give to the winds thy fears;
hope and be undismayed;
God hears thy sighs and counts thy tears;
God shall lift up thy head.
Through waves and clouds and storms
He gently clears the way.
Wait thou His time, so shall the night
soon end in joyous day.[6]

HOPE FOR THE HOPELESS

The hope of Christ can make the everyday hardships a time of joy. This joy goes beyond superficial happiness. At the beginning of this chapter I mentioned two people whose hopes lay in the wrong place. Rick and Teresa need to challenge their perception of their trials and realize that their hope is false because it is placed in the eventual end of the hardship. The hope God wants the Christian to have lies in realizing that in the *midst* of the trial there is a living hope. When trials are perceived properly, then they will perform their work of molding and making us more like Christ.

A preacher has to wear many hats to run a ministry, and I have had to wear a hard hat on more than one occasion. Our church has built all of its own buildings, and the Lord has blessed those efforts. However, these times were also fraught with difficulty. They were times when we as a church had to learn to trust in God's living hope.

Our latest building is bigger than anything we had attempted before (76,000 square feet!). We also were building this time with a material we had never used before—steel. In all of our other construction efforts, we used wood to frame out the construction.

When we ordered the steel, the company assured us that it would arrive promptly. Anticipating a typical cold Chicago winter, we wanted to get the building enclosed before it got too cold to work outdoors.

Our volunteer crews worked hard getting ready for the steel to arrive. Then we heard it would be delayed by a week. We didn't worry about it too much. Several weeks went by. After repeated promises by the company, we began to lose faith. We realized that it was crucial that the steel get there in order for us to finish on time. A month went by, then another. The weather started to turn cold. The leaves were off the trees. Snow gently blanketed the ground.

One Monday morning, just as we were about to give up hope, the steel arrived. Nine semi-trucks pulled into our parking lot. We had been waiting for this moment for fourteen weeks. There was so much steel that it took an entire day just to unload it off the trucks.

The next morning we began placing the columns. This part of the project went remarkably well. But as we bolted together the steel beams, we were amazed at how gigantic they really were. They resembled huge airplane wings. Each one was 120 feet long and weighed 8,000 pounds.

Having never done anything of this magnitude before, we ordered a 125-ton crane to help us set the beams. The owner of this crane came out a few days before we were ready to put them up. Paul Julian, one of the essential people in organizing the work crews, remembers talking to him. "He [the owner] looked at the beams stretching across the concrete foundation and said he thought there wouldn't be a problem," Paul said. "He mentioned that he would have his driver bring a spreader, and that would help lift the massive beams."

A snowstorm hit the night before that decisive day of setting the first beam, leaving four inches of snow in its wake. Before the crews could even begin, they had to shovel all of the snow out of the way. The biting wind tore at our faces, and when I looked at those huge pieces of steel, I realized that it would take more faith than I possessed to get even one of them off the ground.

The driver and the crane arrived. Right away I sensed he had a different attitude toward this project than the owner of the crane. He seemed uneasy about trying to lift such huge pieces with only one crane. Paul asked him about the spreader, and the driver said he hadn't brought one, and even if he had, it wouldn't have helped.

Trying to keep down the disappointment I was feeling was difficult. With the complexity of getting a permit for this project and now after waiting two and a half months for the steel to arrive, it looked like this building would never be built.

The crane operator was willing to try in spite of his misgivings. He started the crane and helped hook up the first beam. Praying silently, I watched the crane slowly lift it. For a foot or so the beam lifted fine. Then in the worst nightmare of my life, the huge piece of steel began to flop and twist. The danger to the crew below was great, and I quickly gave the order for the steel to lower. In spite of that piece of steel being stronger than any other building material, if it could not be lifted properly, it would twist. Imagine holding a piece of cooked spaghetti in the middle and seeing the ends sag. That is what happened to the ends of that beam.

The driver recommended renting another crane, but we knew that would cost too much. Also we wondered whether our foundation could handle two such cranes. Besides, we would have to wait for another one to be available. We had been waiting so long for the steel to arrive, and that made this blow seem even crueler. I looked at all the men standing around. The disappointment in their eyes was great.

The hopelessness I felt at that moment is hard to describe, and I needed to be alone with God. For a moment I did what all of us do when faced with an impossible situation. I wanted to quit. I felt like walking away from the whole project and saying, "Sorry, men. This is much harder than I bargained for. I can't do it anymore." My heart had sagged the moment I saw that steel sag.

Then I noticed that the crews had gathered in small groups.

Their heads were bowed. I knew they were praying. We had experienced many such moments of placing the building project in the Lord's hands, but this moment was the most desperate.

I cried out to God. "I place this project in Your hands, Lord," I said. "I don't know what to do anymore. You will have to show us the way."

Several of the main crew and I got together. We prayed. Then we talked through the process. Since none of us had ever worked with steel in this massive size before, the solution wasn't immediately clear . . . except, what about trying to brace the steel in some way in the middle while the crane lifted the sides? If we could keep the tension perfect, it might just work. I felt a slight glimmer of hope. I wanted to believe the idea would work, but I didn't have much faith. We attached the crane to two points on the beam equidistant from the ends. We then attached two come-alongs to the midpoint. A scissor lift was brought over, and the cables from the come-alongs were attached to it.

With men standing on lifts near the top of the columns ready to bolt the beam into place, the crane slowly lifted. The middle started to sag, but this time we were ready. The men quickly cranked the come-alongs until the tension was firm all across the beam. As the big crane lifted the beam a little more, immediately the men cranked the come-alongs. It seemed like an eternity, but in about twenty minutes, the beam was bolted securely in place.

A cheer broke out. I felt great relief. Somehow I knew the instant that beam had been bolted into place that the building would be finished on time. By the second day, all ten beams were in place, and the work of covering the structure began.

Walking through the different areas of our now-completed building, I reflect on the difficulty we experienced. There probably wasn't a single day in the entire venture that some hardship didn't arise. Those hardships turned out to be opportunities for

God to show His glory. Now a beautiful 2,500-seat auditorium and multipurpose facility stands as a testimony to God's grace.

This same principle is true of our lives. While every day there are going to be times of adversity, these will also be opportunities for Christ to be glorified. They will be times for your own faith to be strengthened as you utilize God's living hope on a daily basis.

Peter also understood this truth. He found that while it was important to be faithful, it was God who would do the building.

When I stand in the pulpit of our new auditorium, I can't help but glance at the beams running across the roof. Every time I see their stalwart strength, I picture them bending like a piece of spaghetti. I remember that in the darkest moment of despair, God sent some of His angels to hold up that beam and get it into place.

Dear friend, what about you? Do the trials and troubles you face seem more than you can bear? Then first realize that hardships are going to be a normal part of your Christian life. In the end you will look back and see that the entire structure of your life was based on that moment you decided to hang onto God's hope.

Take some time right now and decide to hold onto this hope. Don't be tempted to let loose even when nothing is going right. Those are the moments of testing, of trial, and if you hang on, of victory. Just as I saw the strength of God lift that beam and bolt it into place, so He will lift you and hold you in the hollow of His hand.

7

Looking Backward to Look Forward

Once the steel skeleton of our new church building was assembled, the roof then needed construction. When I thought about the expanse the roof had to cover, 250 feet long by 120 feet wide, I was amazed at how big this building really was! Again, none of us had experience with roofing, let alone with steel. I pointed out before that this project took place in the dead of winter. Once the roof was on, filler studs and drywall would enclose the outside structure. The men could then work inside protected from the freezing wind. We anticipated that this part of the project wouldn't take as long as it did to put up the columns and beams.

There were many meetings about the logistics of fitting the roof together, and soon we felt ready. As the men began their ascent in the lifts, I caught my breath. Although they wore safety equipment, fifty feet off the ground is high! Our hopes to complete the roofing were dashed after the first day. Only two panels, each about two feet long, were bolted into place.

I calculated how long the roofing would take if every day went as slowly as this one. My hopes plummeted as I realized it would take approximately a year and a half just to finish the roof! This job encompassed only one small aspect of all we needed to accomplish.

The second day was a little better. Four or five panels went up. On the third day the men started to fly. Thirty panels were placed! Our hopes revived, and I remembered again that just as God had led us every step of the way in the past, so He would continue to lead in the future.

Remembering past blessings is a key toward hanging onto hope. When discouraged, the believer should remember the person who led him or her to Christ or the events that led up to conversion. He should recall how God has led him to the place where he now is. This is why the Christian needs to look backward. Paul writes of this in 1 Thessalonians 2:9: "For ye remember, brethren, our labour and travail: for labouring night and day, because we would not be chargeable unto any of you, we preached unto you the gospel of God." The believers needed to remember the tough trials Paul endured in order to preach the Gospel to them. They needed to thank God that someone cared enough to come and share with them the greatest news they could ever have heard.

Unfortunately, the believer is often better at remembering his past mistakes. He lives sorrowfully in the Realm of Regret instead of graciously in Thanksgiving Territory.

When I realized how long it would take us to finish the roof, I could have become so discouraged that I would have told the men to quit working. If I had continued thinking this way, I would have remembered in rapid succession each difficulty we had encountered. Every discouragement would come to stand before me, pointing its accusing finger. Then I would have gone back to the beginning of my life and dredged up every past personal hurt, revisiting painful memories and reliving every bitter experience.

While it is a human tendency to remember our past mistakes, it takes the work of the Holy Spirit to remember the divine intervention in those times of despair. Can you imagine what would have happened if Peter had done this at Calvary? What if, instead of realizing the Lord's love and care, he had remembered every past failing? While he probably remembered other sins besides his denial, he also came to an understanding of God's love for him.

Before we purchased our first property in Palatine, Illinois, I felt tempted to give in to discouragement. This was several years after coming to live in Chicago. We were meeting at a public school. We desired to purchase land for our future church. We spent a lot of time looking for the right piece of property but could never find what we needed. Everything was either too expensive or wouldn't work. I put an ad in the paper asking if anyone knew of any land that would work for us. Hearing nothing, I was tempted to say to God, "Don't you see that we need property if our church is ever going to grow?"

Instead, I remembered God's steady hand of guidance when He helped us pay our bills month after month. I recalled His faithfulness as our attendance reached 100 people for the first time on a Sunday morning a few weeks before that date. Remembering His faithfulness gave me the courage I needed to wait.

A few weeks later I received a call from a realtor. It seemed that the night before he was going through some stuff to throw away and came across our ad in an old newspaper. He knew of some property and wanted to show it to me. The property turned out to be just what we needed! The Lord miraculously provided us with the funds, and soon we owned a two-and-a-quarter-acre plot of land. It even had a small house where we met until we built. Instead of retreating into depression when it seemed that my prayers weren't being answered, I remembered the goodness of God. Recalling past faithfulness helped me to realize that He cared about my future as well.

The Courage to Begin Again

In the last chapter we studied Peter's living hope. In this section we are going to delve deeper into how this hope can bring those who are humiliated and hurting to fresh faith and power.

A school system in a large city had a program to help children keep up with their schoolwork during stays in the city's hospital.

One day a teacher who was assigned to the program received a routine call asking her to visit a sick child. She took the child's name and room number and talked briefly to the child's regular class teacher. "We're studying nouns and adverbs in his class now," the child's teacher said.

The hospital program teacher went to see the boy that afternoon. A terrible fire had badly burned him, and he was in great pain. Upset at the sight of the boy, she stammered as she said, "I've been sent by your school to help you with nouns and adverbs." When she left, she thought she hadn't accomplished much.

The next day a nurse from the boy's ward asked her, "What did you do to that child?"

The teacher thought she must have done something wrong and began to apologize. "No, no," said the nurse. "You don't know what I mean. We have been worried about that little boy, but ever since yesterday, his whole attitude has changed. He is fighting back, responding to treatment. It's as though he has decided to live."

Two weeks later the boy explained that he had completely given up hope until the teacher arrived. Everything changed when he came to a simple realization. He said, "They wouldn't send a teacher to work on nouns and adverbs with a dying boy, would they?"[1]

There have been many times in my life when my plans were stymied for a while. In the overall plan of God, I see now that those times were actually an opportunity for God to show His power and strength. If I had found our first property easily, then I wouldn't have learned a valuable lesson on waiting for God's timing. If the roofing had gone well the very first day, then we would have thought that it was through our own power that we finished the building. Instead, both of these instances were times when my faith in God grew. That little boy felt justified in having his own personal pity party as he lay in that hospital bed. After all, he was badly burned and in great pain. But the moment that teacher gave him hope, he realized that he could get well.

Are you at a point where you need a fresh dose of hope? Maybe you have sought direction from God, but He doesn't seem to be answering your prayers. Look back on your life. Remember His faithfulness to you in your past. Don't get stuck dwelling on your slip-ups, blunders, and oversights. Consider instead His overriding goodness in spite of your mistakes. Let this backward snapshot encourage you to look forward, eagerly anticipating His hand of blessing!

Hope Even When Humiliated

When the two women came to tell everyone the good news that they had seen the risen Christ, Peter might have hung back from the excited group. He could have thought, *Jesus won't want to see me after what I did*. Then Mary Magdalene might have seen Peter's despondent look and said, "Peter, he specifically mentioned your name! He wanted us to tell you *personally* that He had risen from the dead!"[2]

In his deepest humiliation Peter realized the life-generating hope of the Lord Jesus. He discovered that the Lord still loved and cared enough about him to give him hope again.

If I think about the resurrection of Jesus Christ and look forward to all God has for me, then I too can have a living hope. I am able to cope with life *now*, even in whatever humiliation I experience. Even when I fail, I still possess this hope, because this hope isn't based on my performance. Instead, it is based on the unchanging character of God.

Someone said, "A person can live forty days without food, four days without water, four minutes without air, but only four seconds without hope." Hope is the power that keeps us going in the toughest times. It takes obstacles and transforms them into possibilities. Hope gives us the strength and courage we need to make the most out of life.[3]

Gutzon Borglum was the sculptor responsible for the magnificent rock sculpture portraits of the presidents on Mount Rushmore. In one of his biographies, there is a story about his housekeeper who was quite a fan of his. She was taken to the site before he began his work. And when he finished the work, she was taken again. As she looked up into those faces, she turned to Borglum and said, "How did you know that Mr. Lincoln was in that rock?"

Peter saw his past as only an irregular, unformed piece of rock. Yet the Lord saw His own image in Peter. The Lord looks at us the same way. He is not primarily concerned with where we are now. He sees us in terms of the finished product.[4]

In a single day Job, an Old Testament saint, lost all of his children. Then his wealth was destroyed, and sores covered his body. To add insult to injury, his wife said, "Curse God and die."[5] In my opinion, perhaps part of his trial was his wife!

Yet Job made an amazing statement that shows his eternal hope. He knew something that every one of us should remember: "For I know that my redeemer liveth, and that he shall stand at the latter day upon the earth: And though after my skin worms destroy this body, yet in my flesh shall I see God" (Job 19:25-26).

Just as the hope of the risen Christ sustained Peter, so the hope of his living Redeemer sustained Job. This hope sustained him in spite of his horrific trials. This hope brought strength to his sagging soul. He probably felt humiliated as well. I'm sure the sores that covered his body brought rude comments from those who saw him. I'm sure that since he was once a rich man, the experience of poverty was embarrassing. Yet our Living Hope didn't come to bring healing to those who were whole! He specializes in those who feel humiliated, embarrassed, and disgraced.

I am sure that there have been times in your life when you

could identify with both Peter and Job. The memory of a bitter divorce can keep you from moving forward in your Christian life. Maybe you still feel humiliated when you think of being fired from a past job. It could be that recalling bitter words spoken to a relative still makes you feel embarrassed.

Perhaps, like Peter, you want to cower in the corner because of your failure. But just as the Lord specifically said for Peter to be told of His resurrection, so He wants to assure you of His continuing support and love. Don't let painful memories keep you from growing in Christ. Get involved in a good Bible-believing and teaching church, study the Word of God, find some godly friends who will support you, and witness to those around you. All of these things will bring the realization that God still wants to bring encouragement and blessing into your life.

YOU CAN BANK ON IT

Maggie grew up watching *Leave It to Beaver*, *Ozzie and Harriet*, and other TV sitcoms. She wanted to marry a man who came home at 5:30 every night, live in a nice suburban home, and have beautiful, obedient children. Her life has been very different from the dream she once had. Divorced twice, her adult children haven't seen her for years. On the one occasion her daughter did call, it was to ask for money. When Maggie refused, a big fight ensued. While she was talking with her daughter, Maggie idly flipped the channel on the TV set to an old rerun of *Ozzie and Harriet*. Seeing their idyllic situation, she couldn't help contrasting what had really happened to her life.

Maggie's problem is the same one many Christians have. The treasures of this world might have a superficial brightness. The grass might look greener on the other side of the fence, but who determined that green grass is what you want anyway?

Maggie has a false view of life. Her girlhood dreams will never measure up to her present reality. And so we sometimes carry from our childhood false dreams that haunt even our spiritual expectations.

One writer shares his experience with those who are always looking for "greener grass." He is amazed how often people end up envying the very people who envy them. A pastor sat back in his chair listening to the man seated across from him complain about the cross God had given him to bear. This prominent member of his church was regretting he had chosen his line of work. He knew he should be grateful. After all, since he had bought the majority position in the company, the stock had split twice. The profit-and-loss statements for the last three years had supplied him with excellent Christmas bonuses. He and his wife had enjoyed visits to Europe, the Orient, etc. But at one time he had desired to become a preacher. Instead of finishing seminary, he found a job in the secular world. He went on to outline how much he envied the pastor's knowledge of the Bible and his grasp of theology. He wished that he had time to sit around and read the Scriptures all day. Furthermore . . .

The pastor looked past the man's tailored suit to the window through which he could see the two cars parked outside his study. They were the same color, but that was as far as the similarities could go. As soon as this appointment was over, he would have to take his aging Pontiac home so that his wife could borrow it to do her chores. As his counselee rambled on about what a spiritual loser he was, the pastor studied the picture framed on the corner of his desk. His two children smiled so broadly and so proudly. They were too young to be self-conscious. But in a few years they would realize what he already knew. Their teeth needed elaborate orthodontic work, but it wasn't going to happen on his paycheck. No one knew that money was the biggest temptation of this pastor's life.[6]

No matter what position we are in, whether we are a church leader or a layperson, the temptation to base our lives on material things is all too common. TV ads tout the latest products by showing smiling, good-looking people. The implication is clear. If you use that certain brand of toothpaste or drive that shiny car, then you too will be beautiful and happy.

Maggie has unknowingly bought into that image since she was a little girl. She needs to realize that the problem isn't just that her dreams haven't been fulfilled, but also that her dreams weren't realistic in the first place. Her dreams need to first be based on the reality of Christ. Then once the foundation is secure, she will see that when she chooses to walk each day with Christ, she will finally experience the happiness for which she longs.

There are those who say that a Christian can be so heavenly minded he is of no earthly good. They mean by that statement that Christians should lean at least a little on the world's philosophy and ideals. That way if the Christian life doesn't work, they will still possess a functional worldly viewpoint. The obvious problem with this thinking is that the things of this world are temporary, whereas the spiritual is eternal. If we base our lives even a little bit on that which will not last, then what profit is that for the Christian? Second Corinthians 4:18 states, "While we look not at the things which are seen, but at the things which are not seen: for the things which are seen are temporal; but the things which are not seen are eternal."

The view presented in Scripture is that it's impossible for the believer to be too heavenly minded. The Christian who has the right perspective about the things of this world will be of the greatest use to Christ.

I read about an artist who draws his paintings in the sand and then lets the tide wash them away. He said, "Let the waves wash them away. Images in the sand—that is all life is in the end." This is true even of our dreams about what our lives could have been like. If those dreams have no basis in the reality of the Bible, then those imaginings are going to keep you from experiencing true joy in the living hope of Christ.

So what can the Christian dream about? Peter gives the believer a truth about where his thoughts should center. Look at 1 Peter 1:4: "To an inheritance incorruptible, and undefiled, and that fadeth not away, reserved in heaven for you." This eternal inheritance is incorruptible, which means that it won't be corrupted. It is undefiled, which means that it is pure. And it won't fade with time.

Our living hope is based not only on what we have now (the Holy Spirit, the Bible, direct communication with God through prayer), but also on what lies ahead. Peter knew that God had forgiven him for his past. He also had the living hope of the present, and his future was taken care of because of where he would spend eternity.

This same principle can inspire and help the believer. Your past is settled, your present is hopeful, and your future is secure. Learn today to look to Christ as the Author of your past, present, and future. Realize that He is concerned that your yesterdays don't torment you and that your todays are full of joy. He has lovingly prepared for your future a place of rest and peace.

Floating on Clouds

If you aren't thrilled when you think about your eternal inheritance, then maybe it is because your perception of heaven is skewed. Heaven is not a surreal place. You will feel, taste, touch, smell, and see in heaven. You will experience life to the fullest.

The media has portrayed a picture of this celestial place that is decidedly unbiblical. A place where the pastimes are sitting on clouds and strumming the harp could not be further from the view presented in the Bible. That picture doesn't inspire me to want to go there either!

A Christian writer said, "The caricature of heaven as an eternity of idleness has no basis in Scripture. Instead, the New Testament conception unites the two thoughts of being with Christ and of service for Christ. Remember that if there is to be service there, the exercising ground is here. I do not know what we are in this world for unless it is to apprentice us for heaven. Life on earth is a bewilderment unless we are being trained here for a nobler work which lies beyond the grave."[7]

A little girl was taking an evening walk with her father. With great wonder, she looked up at the stars and exclaimed, "Oh, Daddy, if the wrong side of heaven is so beautiful, what must the right side be!" Think of the most beautiful places in our world today. Look at the sky when you are in the country far away from city life. Since God created this earth with such beauty, it is easy to imagine heaven's splendor.

This hope of heaven is part of our living hope today. Thinking every day of what heaven will be like will help you to walk closer to the Savior. Using opportunities to share with others how to go to heaven will keep you thinking about what is awaiting you. This hope will purify your daily life and prepare you for the hereafter.

A father once shared a story that illustrates how the hope of heaven purifies us now. One day his little boy came into his office. The father watched in amusement as his son rummaged through his desk drawers. Then with great excitement, he pulled out a little pocketknife. His eyes got as big as saucers, and he said, "Oh! Just what I've always wanted!"

The father said, "I'll tell you what, son. I'll give you the knife. We will just put it someplace, and when you are older, you can have it."

So he got a little box for the knife and put it on the top shelf of his closet. He showed the little boy where it was and said, "I'm going to keep it for you."

For weeks after that, whenever the son would get bored or things weren't going well, he would run in and say, "Do you have my knife?" And the father would show him where it was.

Just as the knife had to be kept for the boy until he was older and more responsible, so the believer must wait to receive his full inheritance. Knowing he would someday receive the knife gave the boy encouragement when he needed it. But the promise that guarantees our inheritance is greater than the promise that father gave his son. For we have the Holy Spirit dwelling within us. The Holy Spirit is the earnest of our inheritance (Ephesians 1:13-14).[8] Just as the couple gives earnest money to show they are serious about purchasing their first home, so the indwelling of the Holy Spirit shows us that our inheritance is sure. Looking toward this inheritance will give you strength for the trials you face every day.

An Attitude Adjustment

Think back on the two principles Peter has given for spiritual success.

1) We have a living hope.
2) We have an eternal inheritance.

Using these two spiritual steps for success can give us victory in the trials we know we are going to face.

Peter gives us additional insight into how to have the proper attitude in the midst of trials: "Who are kept by the power of God through faith unto salvation ready to be revealed in the last time. Wherein ye greatly rejoice, though now for a season, if need be, ye are in heaviness through manifold temptations: That the trial of your faith, being much more precious than of gold that perisheth, though it be tried with fire, might be found unto praise and honour and glory at the appearing of Jesus Christ" (1 Peter 1:5-7). If anyone understood how a trial of faith could bring glory and honor to Christ, it was Peter.

I experienced a practical example of this principle after we had completed the roof of our building. Glad the work crews could stay on the ground for a while, I was also torn emotionally. It was time to embark on my annual crusade to India, and while I knew there were people who needed to hear the Gospel, I hated to leave. Reluctantly I boarded the plane along with ten others from the church. It was difficult to call home from the remote area of the crusades, but I did as often as I could.

While I was in India, the crews planned to put in all the filler studs and drywall so the perimeter of the structure could be enclosed. Three walls were erected, and the crews worked hard to finish the fourth.

Since India time is eleven and a half hours different from Chicago time, I called late at night in order to find out the news at church. But I got nervous when the secretaries started playing hot potato with the phone. One said, "Have you heard the news?" When I answered that I had called in order to find out the news, she gave the phone to another secretary. My patience started to wear thin. Obviously there was something wrong.

It was already a miracle to get through from India and stay connected long enough to carry on a short conversation. I couldn't help adding up what this phone call was going to cost as the secretaries tried to decide who should tell me the news.

Finally my daughter Julie got stuck with the phone. Immediately she began to cry. By this time my mind was racing a thousand miles per hour. I was beginning to wonder if anyone in the Chicago area was still alive!

I tried to be patient. "Julie, what's wrong?" I asked.

She told me then that Ralph Kawolski had suffered a fatal heart attack the night before. Ralph was the second original member of our church. His death was just as difficult for me as losing someone in my immediate family. Although I was comforted that he was with the Lord, I mourned that never again would I hear his cheerful, "Hi, Pastor!"

Just as I began to recover from this first blow, Julie passed the phone to my project manager, Dave Lively. He dropped bomb number two. The night before, just as he was leaving, he noticed something strange about the third wall of the building. Terrible winds from the east had whipped into the three walls of the structure, which in effect became a wind tunnel. All the filler studs and drywall in the west end were ripped out.

I was devastated, unable to help physically because of the crusades. Then I remembered Peter's principles for spiritual success. I remembered the goodness of God in the past. I possessed a living hope for the present, and my future was secure. I encouraged Dave to continue with the excellent job he and the men were doing.

It was a tribute to our work crew's trust in God's strength, for they were undaunted by the delay. Less than a week of time was lost. The third wall was rebuilt, along with the fourth, bringing the project to a place where it could really take off.

Before this point we hadn't been able to use fully the people of the church. Putting up beams and columns of steel was specialized work that we could only train a few to do. But after the building was enclosed, the church could mobilize its forces and pour all of its manpower into finishing the job. The wall blew out in early January, and by September of the same year, we held our first service there. As I stood in the pulpit of the new auditorium that first Sunday morning, I praised God for giving me the strength to look backward and remember His goodness. Then I thanked Him for His continuing help for the present. I remembered too that this life with its wonderful blessings from our heavenly Father is just a shadow of the wonders awaiting us in glory.

We can all learn these continuing principles for spiritual success. Do you need to look backward and remember God's faithfulness? Then do this so you can look forward expecting God's unceasing guidance. If you keep in mind His protection in the past, His present living hope, and your eternally secure future, then you will gain a new vision of His purpose. The strength of this truth will carry you safely through every tomorrow.

8

Holiness Is Not What You Think It Is

Because the district superintendent was directly over my father in leadership, he often stayed at our house when he was in town. Bishops were next up the hierarchy, and we didn't get to see them frequently.

One year Dad received the honor of being the host pastor for the annual conference. The bishop stayed at a local motel. Toward the end of the conference, I learned that he had some serious drinking problems and did not behave very well. This did not do much for a twelve-year-old's respect for the hierarchy of the church.

Since I have been a pastor, probably the hardest thing I combat is people's acquaintance with "religious hypocrites." Perhaps a preacher let them down, or a churchgoing relative hurt them in some way. Anyone who claims to be religious is subject to certain expectations regarding behavior. When these people let friends and loved ones down, they hurt more than just their own lives. While the American people say they don't care how the President lives, I believe they are still bothered by how their pastor conducts himself.

The problem is that we have a false view of holiness. Every culture and religion strives for holiness, but even the best intentions can't come close to God's standard.

"Wash away your stress, heal your pain, and cure disease," promises an Internet site that offers a week at a resort in Bali, Indonesia. What caught my eye is the story told about this retreat.

It seems that around the year A.D. 1300 an Indian holy man, or sadhu, was traveling through Bali teaching the secrets of the Hindu tradition. During his journey he became ill at that site. A Balinese spiritual healer "miraculously" restored the man to health. In this instance it appears that it is the "holy man" who makes the site holy.

Hindu sadhus, Buddhist monks, Islam marabouts, Eastern Orthodox monks, Roman Catholic orders—almost every religion has individuals who seek to become "perfect" by asceticism. They retreat from the outside world and renounce all worldly comforts while focusing their thoughts on God.

In some ways, it would be nice to retreat instead of resist. The influences of the culture around us are difficult to ignore. Network ratings go up if TV shows shock viewers. Unusual ad campaigns focus on the bizarre. Radio talk shows have people saying anything and everything on the air. Does this mean we have to move away from these influences in order to become holy?

Isolation assumes that the problem is environmental. There is no question that our contaminated culture pounds its influence home every day that we are exposed to it, but retreating from it all isn't the answer.[1] While I believe in separated living for the Christian, the Bible also teaches that we are in the world but not of it. We don't have to place our sin natures or our children's sin natures in evil situations. We can keep the gasoline of the world from adding fuel to the fire of the flesh. But no matter how hard we try, we can't retreat from the sin nature that is inherently a part of us.

Anyone Can Be holy?

To experience spiritual success, it is important first that you learn God's standard of holiness. While most people equate holiness with certain occupations, the Bible is clear that anyone can be holy. Our good deeds have nothing to do with how God sees us. Before we trusted Christ, we were dead in sin (Ephesians 2:1). No matter what we did to try to earn God's favor, nothing could change the fact that we were already condemned. It only takes one sin to separate us from an absolutely holy God.

Christ's payment on the cross brought reconciliation between sinful people and their holy God. Therefore, it is not what a person does that earns this grace; it is what Christ already did. When people trust in that payment, they can be sure that Christ's holiness covers their sin. Peter understood what it meant to be holy when he put his trust in Christ. Consequently, he realized that it wasn't his good works that made him holy. Rather he became holy in God's sight the moment he trusted Christ's death as the payment for his sin.

Our thinking should start to clear up about holy living once we realize that our holiness is not dependent on our performance. True Christlike living happens when we learn to depend not on our own strength but on the Holy Spirit's power. It is not the external; rather it is the internal.

We have shown how Peter learned this truth at the arrest and crucifixion of Christ. In the fiery trial he denied his Lord. As he wept bitterly, he realized that Christ's love outweighed his sin. That's when he began to rest in that love. His works for Christ after that time were done not out of fear of displeasing the Lord but out of gratefulness for His unfailing love.

A situation a couple faced illustrates this difference in motivation behind what people do. Married only a few weeks, Joan was shocked to discover that David wanted his shirt freshly ironed every morning. She had to iron it just before he put it on so it would still be warm. (Believe it or not, there are people like this in the world!)

Joan tried to be gentle as she said, "I don't have time to iron your shirt in the morning."

David's anger grew as he and Joan talked. "Joan, you iron my shirt in the morning or else!" he said firmly. The fight escalated until finally both withdrew.

After reflection, David had a change of heart. The next morning he approached his wife. "Joan, honey," he said, "no matter what you do, I will still love you. You do so much to make my life comfortable. I appreciate all you do."

The next morning Joan surprised him by getting up early and ironing David's shirt. She even had a smile on her face as she worked.

Joan's motivation changed the instant she realized that David's love wasn't dependent on her performance. This same truth can be applied to the believer. When we realize that Christ's love for us isn't based on the works we do, then we perform acts of service for Him because we want to show our gratitude for His goodness.

Quality Service Guaranteed?

Some believe that once a person becomes a Christian, his or her service is automatic, kind of like an on/off-old-nature-to-new-nature switch. So the only way to tell if people are Christians is by their good works. If they reverted to their old ways, it must mean that they weren't saved in the first place.

This belief creates a false view of holiness. If pastors were guaranteed that all Christians would serve, then their job would be the easiest in the world. All I would need to do is present the Gospel. Then I could go on autopilot and concentrate on other things.

The doctrine of instant sanctification is an intricate part of the theology of some denominations. A preacher I knew years ago informed me that he had been sanctified, and by this he meant that in his earthly body he was now perfect. I in turn informed him that the Bible teaches a progressive sanctification and that while our position in Christ is secure once we trust Him as our Savior, we have to rely on God's strength to gradually sin less.

Since I didn't agree with him, he became angry. Hoping to

make a point, I said, "You aren't acting like you are sanctified or perfect now." Immediately the man's demeanor changed. He calmed down and said, "I understand what you mean."

While the Bible commands the Christian to do good works after salvation, there is no guarantee he will serve. Service requires a conscious day-to-day choice to live by the power of the Holy Spirit. The old nature is still alive and well in the believer (Romans 7:15-21). The difference is that whereas before conversion the believer was dead in his sin with no hope, now within him abides the power to change. Until salvation, he followed his old nature, and so the worldly influence is strong. He must learn to follow the Holy Spirit's leading in spite of his flesh tempting him to do the opposite.

The Christian life is not immediate transformation; rather it is a lifelong process. God will grant deliverance for the things that enslave, though freedom does not come easily. But this deliverance comes because of daily decisions to starve the old nature (staying away from bad influences, etc.) and consciously feeding the new (prayer, Bible reading, attending a Bible-believing church, etc.).

Many Christians don't continue to factor in the power of their flesh simply because they have been serving the Lord for so long. They don't realize that no matter how long they have served the Lord, their old nature is still a part of them. They stop learning to rely on the power of the Holy Spirit and begin to coast in their own strength. When they commit some sin, all those who looked up to them as "holy" are devastated.

Recently I heard about a pastor who brought his computer into a shop for service. One of the members of his congregation happened to work at the store, and while the repairman worked on the machine, he found porn files. The congregation still doesn't understand how this could happen to their spiritual leader. What they don't realize is that the same thing could happen to anyone who takes his or her eyes off the cross. In order to finish the race of the

Christian life, it is important to learn from the apostle Peter some more steps toward spiritual success. His insights might challenge your preconceived notions about holiness.

FINDING RIGHTEOUSNESS RACEWAY

"Wherefore gird up the loins of your mind, be sober, and hope to the end for the grace that is to be brought unto you at the revelation of Jesus Christ; As obedient children, not fashioning yourselves according to the former lusts in your ignorance: But as he which hath called you is holy, so be ye holy in all manner of conversation; Because it is written, Be ye holy; for I am holy" (1 Peter 1:13-16).

Bert and Winnie were driving to a conference for his work. Bert was peeved because Winnie had taken too long getting ready. The baby-sitter was late, and the dog decided to knock over the trashcan. One of the children announced that a science project was overdue, while another explained that she was late for soccer practice. The couple was too exhausted to talk. After a while Winnie realized they weren't anywhere near their destination.

"Bert, do you know where we are?" she ventured.

Bert glowered but didn't reply.

Winnie tried again. "Do you think we should stop and ask for directions?"

"Of course not!" Bert exploded. "What do you think we are—lost?"

No question about it, Righteousness Raceway is hard to find, and many people are traveling in circles looking for it. Like Bert, they don't want to stop and ask for directions.

Coach Peter shares the following three maxims that will steer us through this navigational nightmare.

1) Keep moving.

2) Keep your cool.

3) Keep your eye on the finish line.

READY TO RACE

A track team gathers before the big meet. The coach's first words of advice are simple but important: "Keep moving. Don't stop no matter what distracts you."

Peter gives this same advice to those of us running on Righteousness Raceway. He explains that first we need to gird up the loins of our mind. The believers who received this epistle understood the cultural image. During Bible times an ordinary person wore a basic garment—a long sleeveless shirt of linen or wool that reached to the knees or ankles. Over this he wore a mantle (similar to a modern-day poncho), although he laid the mantle aside for work. He wore the shirt long for ceremonial occasions or at the market, but for active service such as work or war, he tucked it up into a belt at the waist to leave the legs free.[2] This insured that his clothing wouldn't get in the way. Perhaps a modern way of saying it would be "roll up your sleeves." When a man or woman wants to get in shape, putting on the gym clothes is sometimes the hardest part. So it is for the Christian. He needs to be in the proper frame of mind before he can be effective.

So we see the first lesson from Coach Peter is that this girding up is something actively done. He was saying, "No matter what, keep moving!" The idea of readiness for action is seen in virtually every other instance of this expression in the Bible. Elijah girded up his loins and outran Ahab to Jezreel (1 Kings 18:46). Gehazi was told by Elisha to gird up his loins, take Elisha's staff, and hurry to the Shunammite's son who had died (2 Kings 4:29).

Girding up one's loins is that preparatory action that makes a person ready to take action and move about freely without hindrance. It is important that we are unencumbered from the things that distract us from doing right. When our thinking is in order, the entangling doubts, fears, and reservations will be gone.

Think about when your car gets a flat tire and you put on the spare. It is tempting to continue driving on the spare because it is inconvenient to fix the flat. Yet when the spare gets a flat, you are really in trouble.

It is the same way in the Christian life. We need to handle the things hindering our walk with Christ. We need to fix those flat tires that the old nature and Satan throw our way. And we don't need to fix them with a halfhearted "spare-tire" attempt. We must make a constant effort to keep our minds focused on what God would have us do.

Girding up the loins of our mind could be compared to a runner at his starting block during a race. He looks down and realizes his shoe is untied. Quickly he ties it, finishing just before the race begins. *Whew!* he thinks. *That was a close one!*

Just as that runner needed to make sure his shoes were tied before he started the race, so it is important that the Christian rids himself of those entanglements that will slow him down. Some of these things are easy to recognize. Bad movies, smoking, drinking, profanity—these things are pretty obvious. While they may not be easy for every Christian to change, at least they are easy to identify. In Hebrews it says to lay aside those things that will hinder us, and that passage is not just referring to what we might call the "big sins."[3]

At the University of Kentucky, just after I trusted Christ, I made a decision that has helped me run on Righteousness Raceway. I determined that I would only do things that allowed me to think of Christ. I have found that instead of being tempted to think of Christianity as a list of do's and don'ts, I have focused instead on how to please Jesus Christ. Decisions about what I will or will not do are easy because I have a guideline already established.

This might be where you need to start. Think about the Lord throughout your day. Make every decision in light of what would honor Him. Practice feeding your new nature. Your old nature won't starve to death, but the Holy Spirit will dominate it. Learn to keep the secular and the sacred together in your life. Don't compartmentalize your Christianity into something you just do on Sunday morning. Make it a way of life.

I believe this determination I made has kept me from the danger of legalistic thinking. Webster defines legalism two ways:

1) Strict adherence to law or prescription especially to the letter rather than the spirit.

2) The theological doctrine that salvation is gained through good works.[4]

Legalism is a list of rules that modify only the outward actions but not the inward self. When the Christian's "talk" doesn't match his "walk," he is practicing legalism. God looks on the heart. He is not measuring the Christian's spirituality by a list of do's and don'ts. Rather He sees and understands the believer's motivation. Just because a Christian has standards doesn't mean that he is legalistic. If a Christian is focusing his thoughts on the Lord Jesus Christ, then he will learn to lay aside those things that keep him from spiritual growth. This is not something that happens overnight. It is a process of learning to starve his old nature and feed his new nature every day.

And of course I've already covered the second definition of legalism. The idea of any work possibly helping the believer gain entrance to heaven is both preposterous and contrary to what the Bible says. It is "not by works of righteousness which we have done, but according to his mercy he saved us, by the washing of regeneration, and renewing of the Holy Ghost" (Titus 3:5). God makes it clear in His Word that His Son's blood covers all sin. Nothing that we do can be added to the payment that has already been made.

A Priceless Vow

Around the time I was saved, several other men trusted Christ, and we became friends. I told a friend about my vow to do only activities that would allow me to think of Christ, and he shared that he had made the same promise. Later that week we took two girls from nearby Asbury College to a local movie.

By today's standards this movie wouldn't be considered immoral. But as I sat in the theater, I remembered my vow. It was becoming difficult to think of Jesus Christ. I glanced at my friend and realized he was thinking the same thing. We gently tried to explain to the girls that this movie was hindering our new walk with Christ. We told them that we were going to have to leave.

The girls firmly said they weren't leaving, and so we asked them to catch a ride with another group that was there from Asbury. But just as we were leaving the theater, the girls caught up with us. The only thing I remember about the ride home was that it was extremely quiet.

And yet I had perfect peace. Taking a stand for Christ hadn't been as hard as I thought it would be. I knew as I walked out of the theater that day that I would never go to another movie. And I never have.

This might seem extreme. Some people might even call this legalism. But remember this: The vow I made was something I did on my own. This was before I had even attended a Bible-teaching church. I came from a denominational background where on Sunday you "got saved," but on Monday you "lost" your salvation by living however you wanted to live.

When I learned that I was saved forever and that no matter what I did, the Lord loved me, I began to change willingly. I learned that God gave me the freedom and the power (in the form of the Holy Spirit) to keep from being entangled by the snares and sins of this world.

Perhaps you are in a situation in which you have had to take some stand for Christ. Maybe some seasoned Christians have tried to discourage you in your zeal. Remember that true Christianity is common sense sprinkled with the love of God. Your actions might initially alienate you from others, but in time your love for Christ will draw others toward you.

Determining your standards and boundaries for Christ before a situation arises is an important part of the spiritual process. The girl who determines ahead of time to save herself for her wedding night will be ready when temptation comes. The man who decides to spend more time at church will keep his schedule free. The couple that decides to bring their children to Sunday school will make sure they go to bed at a decent time on Saturday night.

Is there some determination you need to make in order to gird up the loins of your mind? Decide what you need to do to shed the entanglements of this world. Then stick by your decision, and you will be ready when the temptation comes. This decision will help you stay on track in your holiness quest.

A Clear Head

Peter explains another important rule for running on Righteousness Raceway. Keep your cool or "be sober." Remember the verse we studied before: "Wherefore gird up the loins of your mind, be sober . . ." (1 Peter 1:13a). This second hint means that the Christian needs to keep a cool head so he is ready for the times of difficulty. The words "be sober" have the obvious meaning from the Greek of abstaining from alcohol. But they also mean to be discreet and to watch. If girding one's loins is the state of mind that causes one to be physically ready to act, then keeping sober is the mental condition that enables one to act prudently and with a clear head. Peter later exhorts his readers to be clear-headed so they can pray effectively (4:7) and be able to stand against the wiles of the devil, who is out to destroy them (5:8).[5]

The coach says to his track team members, "Keep a cool head," because he knows that in the heat of competition, it is important to stay calm. In the same way, you can't live the Christian life if you don't focus on Jesus Christ. Too many people get carried away with one particular aspect of Scripture while they virtually ignore the rest. It is important for the Christian to learn the whole counsel of God. This second instruction to keep sober prevents the kind of mindless enthusiasm that has characterized some saints through the years. Recently an angry group of people physically attacked some of their pastors. These preachers had misled their followers into believing that the Lord would return on a certain day (something Christians definitely won't know ahead of time!), and the people had sold their possessions, giving all their money to their leaders. This thoughtless zeal can be avoided in our lives when we remember to stay clear-headed.

One of the ways to keep a cool head is to visit regularly an oasis offered you. A marathon known as the Marathon des Sables (Marathon of the Sands) is known as the toughest footrace on earth. Five hundred competitors from thirty countries take part in this annual race. Men and women traverse nearly 150 miles of the Sahara Desert of Morocco over seven days, while carrying all their food, nine liters of water, and gear.

This marathon would be impossible to run without stopping for refreshment. These runners also have to carry their rations with them. The believer also carries his rations with him. In his Bible he will find strength and encouragement for the race ahead. But there is also an oasis offered the believer, one that will bring springs of refreshment to his spiritual journey—the house of God. If you attend a church where the Bible is taught, you will receive strength and courage that will help you continue to run the race.

Roberta and Juan didn't go to Sunday school as they grew up. In high school they thought people who attended church were goody-goodies who didn't have compassion. Consequently, they didn't even want to be married in a church. The justice of the peace married them.

When Roberta's friend from work invited her to visit her

church, Roberta said, "I've never found any use for church. I'm sure it doesn't matter where I worship God."

Norma didn't push the issue but was always there to lend a helping hand to Roberta. She visibly demonstrated the love of Christ. A few weeks later Roberta received a promotion. She wasn't surprised to find out that Norma had recommended it. As Roberta thanked her, she said, "There is something different about you."

Norma took a deep breath and began to tell Roberta about the Lord Jesus Christ. She shared what a difference He had made in her life. Roberta realized that if it made that much of a difference in Norma, then she wanted to accept Christ as well.

In time Roberta and Juan began to visit Norma's church. They have found that the spiritual help they receive benefits them in their day-to-day living.

If you are like Roberta and haven't found much use for church in the past, why don't you give it another try? You will find an oasis of calm at the local church. Refreshed, you will again be ready to run on Righteousness Raceway.

THE FINAL LAP

On one of our most memorable vacations, my wife and I enjoyed boating in the Florida Keys. One afternoon a group of dolphins performed for us. Jumping out of the water, flipping, and doing other tricks, they did all the things people pay to see them do, except these dolphins were out in the wild, and the show was free!

We needed to start home before it got dark. We were farther away from the dock than we had thought. Our seventeen-foot boat wasn't very big compared to the vastness around us. We started back, uncertain now, in the gathering darkness.

Then I remembered a pair of binoculars that I had just purchased. I realized they were light-gathering, able to take advantage of the fading daylight. Those binoculars saved us as we motored back.

The third word of advice we receive from Coach Peter will help us endure when it gets dark the way that pair of binoculars helped me: "Wherefore gird up the loins of your mind, be sober, and hope to the end for the grace that is to be brought unto you at the revelation of Jesus Christ" (1 Peter 1:13).

"Hope to the end for the grace . . . brought to you at the revelation of Jesus Christ" means to keep your eye on the finish line. Turn neither to the right hand nor to the left as you focus your gaze on Jesus Christ. Just as an engaged couple makes all their plans in light of the forthcoming wedding, so every decision for the Christian should be made in the light of eternity.

Peter wants us to understand that our devotion and desire for heavenly things must not be diluted with desire for earthly things. When my wife and I visit the mall, you can be assured that we go there for two different reasons! I go to walk while she goes to shop. One day I decided to do something unusual and let her shop while I got us both some coffee. While I was waiting in line, I noticed that a man's T-shirt was getting a lot of attention. I couldn't help but notice the familiar saying that reflects the thinking of our culture: "He who has the most toys wins." Then some small print caught me by surprise. It said, "But he is still going to die." The only thing that is certain in this world is the grace found in Jesus Christ.

An article about a voyage from San Francisco to Santa Cruz—a twelve-hour sail—illustrates this truth. Around Davenport (one of the points on the voyage), the winds really picked up on this particular trip. The full spinnaker (a type of sail) was up, and the boat was cruising along at fourteen knots. Tacking is very difficult in that kind of wind, so the navigator shouted to the helmsman, "Pick a point of land ahead, let the wind fill that sail completely, and don't take your eyes off that point."[6]

Christians, your point is Jesus Christ! No matter how the winds blow, no matter how the crew members rush to and fro, no matter how scared you feel, pick a point, keep focused on it, and you will arrive at your destination.

Remembering these three points from Peter will help the Christian navigate Righteousness Raceway. Don't forget to:

1) Keep moving. Don't let anything stop you. Prepare ahead of time for those difficult situations that could impede your progress.

2) Keep your cool. Stay clear-headed through regular study of the Word of God and attendance at a good local church.

3) Keep your eye on the finish line. Jesus Christ is our final destination. Don't forget this no matter how tempted you are to fix your gaze on the things of this world.

ARE WE THERE YET?

All of us have heard children say, "Are we there yet?" when traveling on a long trip. This question might annoy parents, but sometimes as Christians, we need to ask it and then realize we aren't there yet. Running on Righteousness Raceway takes patience, time, and work. Let's see what Peter presents as the outcome of all this effort: "As obedient children, not fashioning yourselves according to the former lusts in your ignorance: But as he which hath called you is holy, so be ye holy in all manner of conversation; Because it is written, Be ye holy; for I am holy" (1 Peter 1:14-16).

As we strive to become more like Jesus Christ, our personal lives are bound to become more holy. As we strive to imitate our Father, we are bound to become more like Him.

When my granddaughter Amy was two years old, she played in the sandbox while I talked to my son (her father). I stood with one foot propped on an old stump, and when I looked down, I realized that she was doing the same thing! In the same way, we can learn to imitate Christ's actions.

Becoming Christlike takes time. The old desires will never totally die because the old nature will never die. But we can learn to walk in the day-to-day strength of the Lord. It has been said that learning holiness is like remembering the sea air even in a musty basement. We learn holiness in an alien culture. One thing I have learned to do is pray this prayer: "Lord, I know that in my own strength I can do nothing, but in Yours I can do all things. Help me to make the decisions today that will strengthen my faith in You."

Do you need to pause and reflect? Then take a moment to do so, and by His grace you will find yourself growing and changing into a spiritual man or woman of God. Don't forget in your holiness quest Coach Peter's words of advice. You will then find strength even when you encounter raging roadblocks and damaging detours.

9

HOW PETER OVERCAME HIS INFERIORITY

DURING THE TELEVISED Olympic games I would love to watch the best dodgeball teams compete. Year after year I'm disappointed because they haven't added this sport yet to the lineup. Athletes battle in such off-the-wall activities as water polo, canoeing, and fencing; why not include the exciting sport of dodgeball?

Some of my worst memories of childhood involve the teacher picking the two biggest kids in the class to be the captains and then allowing them to pick teams. My feelings of dread grew as time after time all my friends were chosen before I was. My mood changed on the days we played dodgeball. Everyone began this game on equal footing, and I was good at dodging balls. Sometimes I even managed to win.

Doubtless, most individuals have experienced times when they were picked last for a team. When this happens, a child's already fragile self-confidence is severely tested. And sports aren't always the bad guy in doing this. Popularity contests, elected positions, and special clubs all present situations that embarrass those who already feel they aren't outgoing, creative, or talented enough. And what happens to these average students—the ones like you and me?

Sometimes the very fact that they feel inferior pushes these people to become productive adults. They feel challenged to overcome their past labels by working hard later in life. But deep inside, a little voice taunts them that they aren't as good as everyone else. And whether they admit it or not, they tend to believe that voice.

To my surprise, feelings of inferiority aren't confined to those "average" achievers. It seems that even those gifted individuals whom we would label as successful sometimes feel that, no matter how hard they try, they won't ever attain their own internal standard.

Sometimes even success can increase the likelihood that a person will think he or she should have accomplished more in life. Maybe a man works hard to win a contest at work, but when he does win, his joy is short-lived because the success brings to mind other goals he can't dream of accomplishing. Or the woman who works hard to be "Super Mom" realizes that on most days she is lucky to do the bare minimum. She wonders if she will ever accomplish the lofty goals she has set for herself. Some senior citizens look back on their lives and, in spite of many triumphs, see only the goals they haven't reached.

In psychiatry today an inferiority complex means that an individual has intense feelings of inadequacy, producing a personality characterized either by extreme reticence or, because of overcompensation, by extreme aggressiveness. This term can also mean a lack of self-esteem or a lack of self-confidence.

This feeling of being less than the best was something the apostle Peter faced daily. If psychiatrists had existed in his time, Peter might have visited one just after he denied Christ. The doctor might have said, "Peter, the good news is that you don't have a complex; the bad news is—you are inferior!"

Humanistic philosophy has invaded the church. Unfortunately Christians have begun to go to the wrong source for their help and in the process have begun to absorb the lie that man's problems are environmental and that the solution lies within himself. While certain behaviors can be classified, it is important to understand that the biblical way to react to our feelings of inferiority is far different from the world's way.

How do we know Peter suffered from these feelings? I have found through my own observation that those who act as if they have all the answers constantly come up empty inside. We have noted Peter's difficulty with keeping his mouth shut. In tense situations he was especially prone to be the first to speak. And because he blurted out whatever he was thinking, he often hurt the Lord.

Many Christians seem to enjoy playing spiritual dodgeball. They go everywhere for the answers to their problems except to the place where the answer is. While avoiding the ball might be the key to success in a game, playing spiritual dodgeball is not biblical.

Peter overcame his own feelings of inadequacy, and so can you. Christ's unconditional love finally started to get through. In the verses that we are studying from his book, he reveals what helped him overcome his former mind-set. Learning what helped Peter will give you support to stop playing spiritual dodgeball.

THE FATHER CONNECTION

A story is told of a Spanish father and son who were estranged. The son ran away, and the father set off to find him. He searched for months to no avail. Finally in a last desperate effort, the father put an ad in a Madrid newspaper. The ad read: "Dear Paco, meet me in front of the newspaper office at noon on Saturday. All is forgiven. I love you. Your Father." On Saturday eighty Pacos showed up, looking for forgiveness and love from their fathers.[1]

What if you opened your newspaper to the following ad? "Dear child, I can't wait to see you. I am preparing a mansion for you. Your needs and desires are important to Me. Won't you give Me a call? I love you. Your Father."

The Bible's pages are full of such assurances. Peter explains this in 1 Peter 1:17: "And if ye call on the Father, who without respect of persons judgeth according to every man's work, pass the time of your sojourning here in fear."

First, notice that Peter mentions a magnificent promise for the Christian, the ability to call on God the Father. He understood that overcoming feelings of insecurity depended on understanding the unconditional love of his Father. As he realized this, he stopped trying to earn love. He rested, knowing he was loved with the greatest love ever known. No longer did he have to worry about being picked last.

There are some Bible teachers who say that you can't understand what it means to have a heavenly Father if you had a poor example for an earthly father. Since the majority of people in the world don't have a positive example in one of their parents, it follows then that most people couldn't have an accurate knowledge of what it means to have a heavenly Father. Scripture though doesn't espouse the view of these Bible teachers. God states that He is a father to the fatherless (Psalm 68:5).

Peter further mentions that our corruptible possessions are nothing compared to redemption by the blood of Christ: "Forasmuch as ye know that ye were not redeemed with corruptible things, as silver and gold, from your vain conversation received by tradition from your fathers; but with the precious blood of Christ, as of a lamb without blemish and without spot" (1 Peter 1:18-19).

Peter's own father imparted to him a heritage of trusting in works for his salvation. That tradition was challenged when he began to follow Christ. When he trusted Jesus as his Messiah, he put away the tradition of earning his salvation.

A parent's efforts to leave a heritage to his children, no matter how sincere, are futile compared to God's sacrifice of His Son for us. Therefore, instead of using your own view of parenthood as your view of God, look to God *first*. Use God's design for fatherhood and motherhood as your master plan. God's great concern and love can overcome any bad parental experiences the Christian has had.

This new way of thinking frees you from the poor examples of parenthood. It helps you to refocus on God's heavenly characteristics and His unconditional love. And this focus is the first step toward overcoming feelings of inadequacy.

After Hitler annexed Poland, the Nazis came to a village to round up Jews. A Christian woman was shopping near a train station where German soldiers loaded Jews destined to die in a concentration camp into rail cars. She saw a soldier push a Jewess toward the station. A little girl toddled behind. He demanded, "Is she your daughter?" The terrified mother looked straight into the other woman's eyes and said, "No, the child is hers." From that moment the Christian woman took that Jewish girl as her own daughter. In the same way, God's grace claimed us for His own. Sending His Son to die for us is absolute proof of that love.

Are you stuck in the rut of viewing God as you view your own father? The best parents can't measure up to our heavenly Father. Free yourself of possible misconceptions caused by a parent's actions by looking to God and calling Him your Father. You will find Peter's first step toward overcoming inferiority beneficial in your own journey.

No One Has a Corner on God

Peter goes on to explain that since you can call God your Father, you can be sure that you are viewed with love. Remember 1 Peter 1:17: "And if ye call on the Father, who without respect of persons judgeth according to every man's work . . ."

God treats every believer as a parent might treat a favorite son or daughter. He regards every person with the same great love. He gives no special treatment regardless of race, nationality, or socioeconomic status. His relationship with you is special and unique because of this perfect love.

Some might argue this and say, "If God treats everyone the

same, then what about Peter, James, and John?" While these men were Jesus' closest disciples, He didn't treat them as His favorites. God will judge the disciples just as he will assess us—on the deeds we have done, whether they be good or bad (2 Corinthians 5:10). God deals equitably with all people. The unbeliever is judged for his unbelief, and the believer is judged for deeds done for Christ.

The Jews who received Peter's epistle tended to think otherwise. They presumed that since they were God's chosen people, they would receive special treatment. Peter is assuring them that the plodder, the sprinter, and the walker in the Christian race are judged on the same basis—what they have done for Christ.

The principal of my high school honored my dad by asking him to speak at my graduation. Being a typical teenager, I told some of my friends that I was planning to visit the World's Fair in New York during the time of commencement. I'll never forget the day the principal called me into his office. He sternly informed me that I would be disappointing the whole school if I didn't come to graduation, especially since my dad was the speaker. I found myself immediately changing my plans, and I'm glad for my father's sake that I did.

Being the preacher's son didn't change the fact that I needed to uphold the same standards as everyone else in the school. It is the same way with God. Each man and woman is treated the same. This knowledge helps me to serve the Lord, especially when I am tempted to compare myself to others. It is easy to think, "Lord, I could do so much more for you if I were only taller or more eloquent."

Yet the powerful truth that God is no respecter of persons changes my perspective. Whether I serve the Lord shouldn't be dependent on my stature, my looks, my ability, my talents, or my possessions. Because the Lord looks at all of us the same, He accepts me the way I am. This approval makes it an easy choice to serve Him. Here is Peter's second principle for overcoming inferiority: God accepts you the way you are. He doesn't compare you with others or expect you to become like anyone else.

Perhaps you have always taken other people's expectations upon yourself and tried to live up to impossible standards. The reality of the Lord's acceptance will free you from the chains of man's approval. God specializes in working with those who are workable. You were the object of His love long before you did anything for Him.

Take a moment and lean on the Lord's approval. You will never have to worry about Him saying, "I wish you were like Brother Bob; that man really could speak in public." Or, "You should sing like Sister Serena; she really knows how to sing praises to Me." The Lord accepted your talents and abilities when He accepted you. If you can believe this truth, you will make great progress toward spiritual rest and peace.

Is Fear Wrong for a Christian?

When thirteen-time U.S. champion diver Mark Ruiz was young, his mother noticed that he enjoyed jumping from the side of the pool more than he enjoyed swimming. His swimming instructor recommended diving, and he never looked back. He is known for his smooth entries into the water and has gained a reputation for consistently ranking at or near the top of competitions. One thing might surprise you about Ruiz. He has a deathly fear of heights.

"Diving is a very fearful sport," he said. "To be a diver you really have to have guts and dedication."

Ruiz doesn't let his fear of heights slow him down. It is actually his fear that propels him to work harder at diving. His fear helps him concentrate on his technique as he stands on the diving board.[2]

Look at Peter's third principle for overcoming inadequacy: "And if ye call on the Father, who without respect of persons judgeth according to every man's work, pass the time of your sojourning here in fear" (1 Peter 1:17).

Does Peter mean that the Christian must cower in the corner afraid to try anything? On the contrary, just as a fear of diving actually propelled Ruiz to do his best, so a fear of God can drive us to selfless acts of service.

The fear of God is compatible with both faith and hope. Faith requires fear. How can we put our trust in a God whom we do not fear? The fear of God is rooted in who God is, in his holiness, power, majesty, justice, and mercy. How could we trust in a God who is not infinitely greater than we are?

Hope looks forward in time and fear does too. Hope looks toward our heavenly inheritance, while fear looks toward the judgment of God. The believer's judgment involves rewards for his faithfulness to Christ.

While at a gym, my youngest granddaughter, Amanda, wanted to walk on a balance beam. We knew she couldn't do it by herself, so her mother (my daughter Julie) lifted her up. Julie held one hand, and I held the other. Because of our help, she walked the length of the beam. The comparison is clear. Hope holds on to one of our hands and draws us toward the things of God, and a healthy fear of God holds the other hand, repelling us from the things that offend Him.

Fear Is a Delight?

Today's "positive thinking" philosophy has pervaded the pulpits of our country. Preachers and Bible teachers don't want to offend people by speaking of "fearing God." Yet the fear of the Lord is healthy and wholesome, leading to blessing and security. While it is our duty to fear God, it is also a delight.

Too many preachers today portray God as a benign being who doesn't demand justice. But while God has granted us the privilege of calling Him Father, He had to sacrifice His own Son to do it. His holiness is so great that His justice demanded the ultimate price. "A son honoureth his father, and a servant his master: if then I be a father, where is mine honour? and if I be a master, where is my fear? saith the LORD of hosts unto you . . ." (Malachi 1:6).

Black Bart was a professional thief whose name struck fear as he terrorized the Wells Fargo stage line. From San Francisco to New York, his name was synonymous with the danger of the frontier. Between 1875 and 1883 he robbed twenty-nine different stagecoach crews. He did this without ever firing a shot. Because a hood covered his face, no victim saw his features. He never took a hostage and was never trailed by a sheriff. Instead, Black Bart used fear to paralyze his victims. His sinister presence was enough to overwhelm the toughest stagecoach guard.[3]

Black Bart preyed upon other people's fear in order to accomplish his evil goals. Yet if you had a proper fear of God, you wouldn't even have to fear Black Bart. The fear of God enriches our lives. It establishes boundaries and helps us to embrace godly living. For it is not God who makes us fear Him. Instead, we make the decision to fear Him. William Gurnall said, "We fear men so much because we fear God so little."

The fear of God frees us from yet another shackle of inferiority. It helps us to focus on what God thinks of us rather than on what man thinks. The Christian who focuses on pleasing God rather than others will learn to be the best servant of Christ.

A man named Adam learned this the hard way. Always an overachiever, he worked hard to make others happy. He didn't realize that he did this as a mask for his own feelings of inferiority until one day a hoped-for promotion failed to come through. Every feeling of inadequacy he had had since childhood came back to torture his mind. His job performance slipped, and just before a scheduled meeting with his supervisor, he came to me for some advice.

I explained these truths to Adam. No matter how much he

worked, there was no way he could totally satisfy other people's expectations. I showed him Peter's principles of accepting the unconditional love of the heavenly Father, realizing that God is no respecter of persons, and cultivating a healthy fear of God rather than man.

When Adam realized that his standing in God's eyes wasn't affected by his own performance, it was as if a great burden rolled off his back. He said with tears in his eyes, "I never realized how much God loved me. I have been trying to perform a certain way in order to gain God's approval, but I realize now that God accepts me for who I am."

After that, Adam stopped using other people's approval or disapproval as the gauge of his own worth. He found that learning to please God is infinitely easier than trying to please those around him all the time.

The Only Fair Judgment

In his book *Mornings on Horseback*, David McCollough tells this story about young Teddy Roosevelt. His mother found that he was so afraid of the Madison Square Church that he refused to set foot inside it alone. He was terrified of something called the "zeal." He said it was crouching in the dark corners of the church ready to jump at him. When she asked what a zeal might be, he said he wasn't sure, but he thought it was probably a large animal like an alligator or a dragon. He had heard the minister read about it from the Bible. Using a concordance, she read him the passages containing the world *zeal* until he told her to stop. The line was from John 2:17: "And his disciples remembered that it was written, The zeal of thine house hath eaten me up."

It is humorous to think of Roosevelt's conception of "zeal" as a dangerous animal. But it is true that our God is a consuming fire. He will execute righteous judgment upon the earth.

And while the believer never has to fear that his judgment will be hell, he does need to understand that he will be judged for his works. The judgment seat of Christ is called the *bema* seat in the New Testament. At the Greek Olympics, rewards were given at a literal *bema* seat to those athletes who excelled. In the same way, when we stand before the judgment seat of Christ, we will receive rewards for the works we have done. This godly fear of His judgment helps us to stay on track and finish the race.

Many modern Christians think that Peter should have written encouraging the early believers to spend their time in comfort and peace. Didn't Peter understand that it is important to eradicate all negative thinking? Instead, Peter offers fear as the solution to our time of sojourning. We should fear evil because our sin is what put Jesus on the cross. This fear Peter talks about is not a fear of torment but rather a daily fear that purifies our lives.

Think of fear as an armed guard watching over your joy in Christ. If you distrust yourself and watch every step while you rest in the hope of your eternal destination, each action will be safe.

Does your fear of God help you to pursue holiness on a daily basis? I challenge you to rethink the role of godly fear in your life. Just as Peter realized that fear was an essential part of helping him pursue the way of the cross, so can you. Just as my Amanda hung on to both Julie and me as she balanced, so you can decide to hang on to both hope and fear. Joy and blessing are awaiting you at the end of the beam; won't you take the first step?

How Much Does It Cost?

If Linda shows me a dress at the store, she might ask, "Do you like it?" Being a typical male, before I can answer her question, I have to ask one of my own: "How much does it cost?" (If you had an illusion that I was a perfect husband, then I'm sure you don't anymore!) I have a hard time telling her my opinion if I don't know how much the dress is going to cost me.

When Adam and Eve sinned in the Garden of Eden, God knew immediately what it would cost Him to redeem man. Yet it is easy to lose sight of the price that was paid for us. Peter in a sense did not appreciate the cross until he realized the price Christ paid for his sin. Although a true appreciation of the cost of the cross can never be attained until heaven, Peter understood more than most the price that had been paid. Because he witnessed the crucifixion, he held a reverential gratitude for his salvation. And because Peter had witnessed personally God's forgiveness in spite of his great sin, he often wrote about grace. In the next verses Peter shares more about this.

"Forasmuch as ye know that ye were not redeemed with corruptible things, as silver and gold, from your vain conversation received by tradition from your fathers; But with the precious blood of Christ, as of a lamb without blemish and without spot" (1 Peter 1:18-19).

Frank is at a crossroads in his life. Arriving almost daily in his mailbox are scholarship offers from major colleges. Science and math are his forte, and his grade point average in high school proves that. Frank recently turned on the radio and heard a preacher explain the ultimate price Jesus paid for him. Although he had grown up in a Christian home, somehow he had never realized just how much he was loved. Hearing about a small Bible college where he could learn more, he finds himself torn. His goal was to become a great engineer, but now he thinks that Christ wants him in full-time ministry.

While Christians in any profession can serve the Lord just as much as those in full-time ministry, the dilemma Frank faces is not unique. When we receive God's call upon our lives, it changes our perspective on what we once perceived as success.

The world's view of success doesn't include Christ's blood.

Rather the only view society has of success depends on what the Bible calls corruptible things, or things that don't have eternal significance. The idea is that if you can only get enough money or material blessings, you will be counted as a success. Someone said that we live in an age where we know the cost of everything and the value of nothing.

But the Bible consistently counters this view by explaining that we are to count the precious blood of Christ as having the highest value. The poorest man isn't a failure if he has accepted the blood of Christ. When will we begin to understand that silver, gold, money, and fame cannot possibly satisfy? "Neither by the blood of goats and calves, but by his own blood he entered in once into the holy place, having obtained eternal redemption for us" (Hebrews 9:12).

AB negative blood is considered the most rare blood type. But as rare and precious as this blood is, Christ's blood is the only blood that can cover our sin. A proper understanding of the price He paid for you will help you understand just how precious you are in His eyes.

Do you want to find out how successful you are in God's eyes? Then ask yourself this question: What is more precious to me, the blood of Christ or silver and gold?

Many years ago at a summer camp program, a young woman came forward during one of the services to dedicate her life to Christ. She later shared her testimony. She said that before she dedicated her life, she found herself dreading it when anyone requested the song "I'd Rather Have Jesus." She found she couldn't sing the following familiar words.

> *I'd rather have Jesus than silver or gold,*
> *I'd rather be His than have riches untold. . . .*
> *I'd rather have Jesus than anything this world affords today.*

She knew she wanted silver and gold more than she wanted Christ. This realization jarred her into thinking about what really mattered. Since she made the decision to follow the Lord, she has touched countless lives with her testimony of grace.

The silver and gold test can help you to determine your priorities. Peter understood how important it was to remember the high cost of his own salvation. If you would choose silver and gold, then you can be assured of heartache and havoc. On the other hand, if you want Jesus more than anything else, then you are sure to realize, like Peter, that you can rest securely and contentedly in the arms of the Savior.

Helpful How-to's

Look again at the steps Peter takes us through to overcome inferiority.

1) He realized that God was his Father.
2) He knew that God accepted him for who he was.
3) His fear of God kept him from evil.
4) Daily he chose Jesus over silver and gold.

Friend, if you take these principles from Peter and apply them to your life, then you too can experience his same life change. Peter found it a freeing experience to take off the shackles of other people's expectations and clothe himself in God's acceptance. You too can experience this freedom when you realize that only God is your judge. He is the One who will enable you to live for Him. He is the One who loves you unconditionally. And He is worth far more than silver and gold.

10

How to Be Purified When You Are Petrified

TWO THEOLOGICAL STUDENTS, each taking a course in Christian living, walked along a street in the Whitechapel district, a section of retail stores and consignment shops in London. One of the students pointed to a suit of clothes hanging in a window. A sign on it read: Slightly soiled—Greatly reduced in price.

Struck by the thought that this was a perfect illustration for a paper he was writing, one of the students said, "We get soiled by gazing at a crude picture, reading a coarse book, or allowing ourselves a little indulgence in dishonest or lustful thoughts; and so when the time comes for our character to be judged, we are greatly reduced in value. Our purity, our strength is gone. We are just part and parcel of the shopworn stock of the world."

As that student realized, no matter what our profession is or the number of years we have known Christ, it is easy to be careless about what we term the "little" sins. Small continual slips from Righteousness Raceway greatly reduce our usefulness. These secret sins weaken our character so that when we face a moral crisis, we can't stand up to the test.

Peter learned this lesson well. He explained that purity in the Christian's life has to be a *priority*. Purity coupled with a healthy fear of God will keep the believer safe. Remember that the fear of God and a hope of heaven balance the Christian experience. Peter learned that when he was petrified, he would be purified.

When a parent sets up rules, it isn't because he wants to spoil his children's fun. On the contrary, these rules provide freedom because they clarify what is acceptable and what is not. My two grown children have shared with me that when they were teenagers, they felt the trust I placed in them was sacred. They didn't want to break the fellowship and enjoyment we all had in one another, and consequently they had no problem following the rules.

It is the same way in the Christian life. When a believer chooses to live by God's standards, he or she will enjoy fellowship with God. A quest for purity will inevitably draw the Christian closer to God. The older I become in Christ, the more aware I am of my sins. Forced then to draw closer to Christ, I realize that His adequacy more than compensates for my own inadequacies. I confess those things that separate me from Him and have Him wash my feet. Peter knew this truth in a deeply personal way and had learned to go to Christ every moment for strength.

The Little Sins Are Out to Get You

Peter remembered that what made Judas fall away from the Lord was what we might term a "little sin," the love of wealth. But in a materialistic culture we reason, *Surely the Lord isn't against those who wish to obtain material possessions or a healthy bank account!*

I've heard preachers say that anything you desire, the Lord will give you. A speaker once used Psalm 37:4 as a reference: "Delight thyself also in the Lord; and he shall give thee the desires of thine heart."

This speaker was interpreting this verse according to his own desires rather than seeing what God really had to say. When a man's or a woman's delight is in the Lord, his or her desires will become like the Lord's desires. While God isn't against giving the believer material wealth, certainly that is not His main desire! Judas' love for money led him to betray the Lord. While this sin might have seemed small when he was the treasurer of the group, his sin grew deep roots in his heart.

Martin looked the part of the good Christian. He wore a suit, carried a Bible, and greeted the new people who came into the church every Sunday. But exposure to a pornographic magazine when he was in junior high left him with a lifelong obsession. He had never dealt with his sin because he thought he couldn't change, and to him it wasn't that bad.

But with his marriage threatening to come apart at the seams and his children on the brink of adolescence, he realized that his hidden sin was causing spiritual strangulation. He took the first bold step by burning his secret stash of magazines. But Martin will need to continue to work toward purity. Getting rid of the source of his temptation is a critical first step. Learning to control his wayward thought life will be much harder.

Now when he travels on business, he calls the hotel's front desk and asks them to cut off the "adult" TV channels. He puts a picture of his wife and kids on top of the TV and even goes so far as to place the remote control outside the room. He has learned to go daily to Christ and confess his sins, including even his thoughts. Because of his sin, Martin was separated from true fellowship with Christ, and this was affecting his relationships with his family. Now that Martin has confessed his sin and is taking active steps toward controlling it, he can grow in his spiritual walk and begin to rebuild his closest relationships. Peter's principles will give him practical suggestions as to how to do just that.

PRACTICAL PURITY

Peter continues to give us practical ways to overcome spiritual failure: "Seeing ye have purified your souls in obeying the truth through the Spirit unto unfeigned love of the brethren, see that ye love one another with a pure heart fervently" (1 Peter 1:22).

If we allow the Spirit of God to work, we will learn to obey the truth, which will purify us daily. Sometimes people make it around the first lap or so of Righteousness Raceway, but then they lose steam. Their quick pace slows to a jog that decelerates to a walk that soon brakes to a stop. And while some people think they can stand still in the Christian life, what they don't realize is that no progress means regression. When there isn't a constant push toward Christ, the lure of the world and the flesh usurp the position of master.

How can we avoid this situation? First we need to keep away from the "let go and let God" trap. Why is this phrase a trap? The Christian life is a *union* between the *truth* of the Word of God and the *working* of the Spirit of God. Spurgeon said, "Let the dignity of nature and the brightness of your prospects, O believers in Christ, make you cleave to holiness and hate the very appearance of evil."

When the Christian puts his life on "coast," thinking that God will push him in the right direction, he is deceiving himself. While it is impossible for the believer to live his Christian life without God's help and strength, it is equally impossible for God to work through the Christian unless the believer obeys the truth of Scripture. God supplies the power, and the believer supplies the willingness to let that power work in his life.

A great example of this truth is our latest construction project. Throughout this book, I've given you many accounts of God's miraculous ability to give us the strength to continue. Yet if we had never begun the project, never put our minds to the task, never been willing to put some muscle where it needed to be, the addition wouldn't have been built.

So it was a partnership between the people of Quentin Road Bible Baptist Church and God that put the building together, and it is the same way in the believer's life. When Christians use these principles from the apostle Peter, they will learn to allow the Spirit of God to work, which helps them to obey the truth. Then they will be purified daily. They will possess both the strength and the ability to serve in a manner well pleasing to God.

Friend, take a moment to determine your spiritual fitness level. Have you served God strongly in the past but now find yourself losing steam? Take a moment and reflect on Peter's call to purity. Perhaps a practical way to allow the Holy Spirit more control in your life would be to open yourself up to more biblical influences. Increase the time spent in Bible study or listen to the Bible on tape as you drive to work. Even five minutes will help you to focus on the Holy Spirit's work.

Maybe you need to begin to pray before *every* situation that arises in your day. One author wrote that a turning point came for her when she determined to make no decision without prayer. Adding these suggestions to your daily life will help you strive toward purity.

PURITY'S GOAL

The goal of purity might surprise you. Those who practice holiness on a daily basis will show love for others. This is far from the rigid and unbending view that some have of the Christian life. A purified soul is a loving and compassionate soul. If you are purified, then the love of Christ will be a part of who you are. This love is not a front you put on to impress others. Rather it is a genuine love that seeks the best interests of brothers and sisters in Christ.

This word *love* used in 1 Peter 1:22 is in the Greek *philadelphia*. This kind of love:

- Denotes a warm brotherly affection, the kind evident in a closely knit family.
- Binds one another in an unbreakable union.
- Holds one another deeply within the heart.
- Knows deep affection for one another.
- Nourishes and nurtures one another.
- Shows concern and looks after the welfare of others.[1]

Like the three sides of a triangle, so there are three parts to purity's goal of love. These aspects of giving, forgiving, and outliving join together to bring the believer the full meaning of what God expects when he or she obeys the command to love. The first facet is a *giving* love.

Love Gives

If you are purified, you will give of yourself to everyone, not just to your inner circle of friends. In the world today it is too easy to love only those who look just like us and act just like us. Yet the love of Christ challenges us to actively love those around us, not just those we would naturally choose to love.

Ann and Jessica found out that they were the only believers in their group at work, so they quickly became good friends. One day Ann's secretary quit, and the temporary worker who was hired seemed to have a personal vendetta against Ann and Jessica. Besides regularly gossiping about them to the other employees, Carol made rude comments to both of them about their faith in Christ.

Then one day Ann arrived at the office to find Carol in tears. Ann wanted to ignore the sorrow she saw on Carol's face. After all, Carol had said quite a few nasty things about her. But she had been to church the past Sunday morning and happened to hear me talking about Peter's principles of purity. She knew it was time to overcome her personal problem with Carol and be her friend. Sitting down next to her, Ann encouraged her to share what was wrong. When Jessica arrived, she was surprised to see Ann and Carol conversing. Later the two friends discussed the situation. They agreed that Carol needed to be shown the love of Christ, and in practical ways they began to carry out their resolution. In time, Ann and Jessica experienced the joy of leading Carol to Christ.

Look again at this verse in 1 Peter: "Seeing ye have purified your souls in obeying the truth through the Spirit unto unfeigned love of the brethren, see that ye love one another with a pure heart fervently" (1 Peter 1:22).

Ann and Jessica provide a practical example of how purity in their lives taught them to love others. The adverb *fervently* is found in this form only once in the New Testament. Its forms indicate both eagerness and perseverance. This kind of love needs to be a constant part of what we say and do. First John 3:18 exhorts: "My little children, let us not love in word, neither in tongue; but in deed and in truth."

The idea of love's perseverance further indicates that this is indeed an action. A choice we make. Maybe you've heard someone say something like this: "I just don't love my wife anymore." Or, "I woke up one morning and found I no longer loved my husband." These statements are preambles to a declaration that since he or she doesn't feel love for the spouse, it's time to leave the marriage. The logic seems to be, "Since I no longer love my mate, then I surely cannot be expected to do any longer what love requires of me."

Yet Peter makes it clear that a feeling of love comes only after we *persevere* in love for others. We have all heard that love is not a feeling but an action. But how many of us have really contemplated what that means? Love not only comes *first* as an incentive for obedience, but it comes *last* because of obedience.

Newspaper columnist George Crane tells of a wife who came into his office full of hatred toward her husband.

"I not only want to leave him, I want to get even," she said. "Before I divorce him, I want to hurt him as much as he has me."

Crane suggested an ingenious plan. "Go home and act as if you really love your husband. Tell him how much he means to you. Praise him for every decent trait. Go out of your way to be kind, considerate, and generous. Make him believe you love him. Then tell him you are getting a divorce. Then it will really hurt him."

With revenge in her eyes she exclaimed, "Beautiful! Will he ever be surprised!"

And she did it with enthusiasm, acting "as if."

When she didn't return, Crane called. "Are you ready now to go through with the divorce?"

"Divorce?" she exclaimed. "Never! I discovered I really do love him." Her actions had changed her feelings. Motion resulted in emotion. Proverbs 16:3 illustrates this point: "Commit thy works unto the LORD, and thy thoughts shall be established."

Don't just say you love others; go out and prove it! C. S. Lewis wrote in *Mere Christianity*, "Do not waste your time bothering whether you 'love' your neighbor, act as if you do. As soon as we do this, we find one of the great secrets. When you are behaving as if you loved someone, you will presently come to love him. If you injure someone you dislike, you will find yourself disliking him more. If you do him a good turn, you will find yourself disliking him less."

The surest road to depression is to begin thinking that everyone should cater to your whims and desires. True love thinks of others.

You might think, *The apostle Peter doesn't understand about my husband's mother! She is a pest! She always has an opinion on everything I do, always a pat word of advice that she has never tried. I don't think Peter would have written this if he had known her.*

Or you might be tempted to imagine Peter being acquainted with the class of ten-year-olds you teach. You feel he wouldn't command you to love others if he knew how frustrating it is to teach kids who don't listen.

But Peter doesn't say to love only those who are *easy* to love. In fact, one of the true proofs of the authenticity of your faith is that you begin to love those who are unlovable.

A man in my church described his father's experience of giving love. His dad at fifty years of age had lost his job. A close Christian friend who knew of his loss knocked on his door a few days later. In the envelope handed to him, this out-of-work father found $500. That money was able to help his family until he got another job. That man's dad experienced love in action, which is a demonstration of our discipleship. There are many commands from our Lord to do this very thing. He knew that if the church enjoys fellowship and unity, unbelievers will see that Christ is real.

Are you ready right now to face difficult situations in your life with a love that gives? Not a love that is stingy, not a "gimme" kind of love—but a love that goes the extra mile. Take a moment and write down ways you can share this love with others. Think of your husband or wife who needs your unconditional care. How about those you work with who need to experience what Christ has to offer? What about your own family and friends? How can you show them your love in action? You will find that when you become more like Christ, your love for others and your concern for their needs will continue to grow.

LOVE FORGIVES

I wish it weren't true, but a preacher is prone to offending others. I find that in teaching, preaching, counseling, and administrating there is great potential for me to say the wrong thing. And I have found that there are some people who have a particularly difficult time with a second aspect of love: Love forgives.

The dilemma isn't necessarily confined to preachers. Many professions have great potential to offend others, especially when people are in positions of leadership. Sometimes it is what you *fail* to do that becomes the offense. This has happened to me. I've had people complain, "The preacher didn't visit me in the hospital," when the person didn't bother to let anyone on the ministry staff know he was in the hospital. Sometimes I'm tempted to think, *I can't win, I might as well give up.* This is a typical human response to those who are "easily offended."

Then I remember that although I cannot control what other people do and say to me, I can control my own actions and words. My thoughts don't have to turn inward. I don't have to stay fixed on some petty offense that matters little. Choosing to let this principle of love work in my life, I will learn in a practical way to show love even when it isn't returned. The devil likes nothing better than to make you think there is a barrier when there isn't one.

When you get offended at a rude comment, learn to forgive. Picture the results of forgiving love. It:

- Endures wrong meekly (1 Corinthians 13:4).
- Renounces calling attention to itself (Matthew 6:5).
- Spends time and energy supplying the needs of others (Romans 12:9-10).
- Receives reproofs without animosity and defensiveness (1 Corinthians 13:5).
- Puts away the list of grievances (Ephesians 4:2).
- Rejoices when others prosper and we don't (Romans 12:15).
- Blesses those who curse us (Luke 6:27).

The prevailing thought behind each of these results is the pure motive of forgiving love. This love first gives in order to show love in action. And then this love forgives, showing that it is indeed a vital and necessary part of your life.

One of the keys to having a love that forgives is to prepare ahead of time for offenses from others. When you wake up in the morning, realize that at some point in the day someone will say something hurtful. Decide that an associate will criticize you behind your back. Even someone you greatly respect and admire spiritually (such as your pastor!) might offend you unintentionally. Forgive that person ahead of time. Then when the offense comes, you are prepared. Your outstretched hands of forgiveness will absorb the barb of the insult. And you will discover the important key to developing Christlike love.

Love Outlives

Not only does love give and then forgive, but it out-lives. When the first two aspects of love are developed, the third naturally forms. The triangle is solid.

Rob Gilbert was walking in a residential section of lower Manhattan. He passed a man walking his dog and did a double take because the dog was wearing shoes!

He walked back to the man and asked him the obvious question, "Why is your dog wearing shoes?"

"Oh, the dog's so old that all the padding on his paws has worn off, and the shoes give him the padding he needs," he said. "As a matter of fact, without the extra padding it would be like you or me walking on hot coals."

Fascinated, he asked how old the dog was.

"He's fifteen and a half, and I've had him since he was a pup."

Totally enthused, Gilbert gushed, "That's amazing. What's your secret? You should write a book about how to take care of your dog."

"It would be a very short book because I only have one secret."

"What's that?"

"I really love my dog."[2]

The man had cared for his dog for so many years that the care was no longer a chore; it was a natural part of his existence. If the human heart can care so deeply for an animal, how much greater love could we have for a Christian brother or sister?

When we put feet to our love, when we prepare ahead of time to forgive, our love will persevere. It will stand the test of time. It will be real, and others will recognize that we are different.

That brings me to a supernatural aspect of this love that outlives—loving not only those who are *like* us or who *like* us but also loving those who hate us. Christ used this as the *absolute proof* of love. "For if ye love them which love you, what reward have ye? do not even the publicans the same? And if ye salute your brethren only, what do ye more than others? do not even the publicans so?" (Matthew 5:46-47).

Loving those who hate us is the hardest aspect of love—and the most important. There is no place for hatred in the Christian life. Fervent love should persist in spite of the selfishness of others. Our supreme delight should come from our faithful love toward all people, even those who are our enemies.

A boy named Ted undoubtedly qualified as one of those difficult to love. Expressionless. Unattractive. Even his teacher, Miss Thompson, saw little promise in his work. Ted's records from school read:

> 1st grade: Ted shows promise with his work and attitude but has poor home situation.
>
> 2nd grade: Ted could do better. Mother seriously ill. Receives little help from home.
>
> 3rd grade: Ted is good boy but too serious. He is a slow learner. His mother died this year.
>
> 4th grade: Ted is very slow but well-behaved. His father shows no interest whatsoever.

Christmas arrived. The children piled elaborately wrapped gifts on their teacher's desk. Ted brought one too. It was wrapped in brown paper and held together with cellophane tape. Miss Thompson opened each gift as the children crowded around to watch. Out of Ted's package fell a gaudy rhinestone bracelet, with half of the stones missing, and a bottle of cheap perfume. The children began to snicker. But she silenced them by splashing some of the perfume on her wrist and letting them smell it. She put the bracelet on too.

At day's end, after the other children had left, Ted came by the teacher's desk and said, "Miss Thompson, you smell just like my mother. And the bracelet looks real pretty on you. I'm glad you like my presents." He left.

Miss Thompson got down on her knees and asked God to forgive her and change her attitude. The next day the children were greeted by a reformed teacher, one committed to loving each of them. Especially the slow ones. Especially Ted.

Surprisingly, or maybe not surprisingly, Ted began to show great improvement. He actually caught up with most of the students and even passed up a few. The year ended, and another came. Miss Thompson heard nothing from Ted for a long time. Then one day she received a note saying that Ted was graduating second in his class. A few years later another note arrived with the news that Ted was graduating first at the university. Then one day Ted informed Miss Thompson that he was getting married and wanted her to sit where his mother would have sat. The compassion she had shown that young man entitled her to that privilege.[3]

When we show compassion to all those around us, even those we perceive as slow or undeserving, we will possess a love that outlives. This love will continue to help us persevere as each day we try to become more like Jesus Christ.

Do you need to take these three aspects of love—giving, forgiving, and out-living—and apply them to your life? If you answered this question with a yes, don't feel discouraged. Realize that every Christian can learn to show more love toward others. Remember too that if we allow the Spirit of God to work, we will learn to obey the truth, which will purify us daily. When I am struggling to show the three aspects of love to others, I turn to God in prayer and ask Him to help me show His divine love. My human love is frail and fragile, but His love is stalwart and strong. The secret to loving others is to let His love overpower and strengthen us.

Would you pray this prayer? "Lord, help me to give Your love to the people who come into my life today. Help them to see Your love in me, and give me the wisdom to recognize situations where

I can forgive ahead of time the offenses that are sure to come. Help me to have a persistent love, a love that out-lives."

Love ever gives.
Forgives, outlives,
And ever stands
With open hands.
And while it lives,
It gives,
For this is love's prerogative—
To give, and give, and give.

OXENHAM

11

PETER'S SPIRITUAL SECRET

NASA LAUNCHED THE exploratory space probe Pioneer 10 in 1972. According to Leon Jaroff in *Time*, the satellite's primary mission was to reach Jupiter, photograph the planet and its moons, and beam data to earth about Jupiter's magnetic field, radiation belts, and atmosphere.

Scientists regarded this as a bold plan, for at that time no earth satellite had ever gone beyond Mars, and they feared that the asteroid belt would destroy the satellite before it could reach its target. But Pioneer 10 accomplished its mission and much more.

It swung past the giant planet in November 1973, and then Jupiter's immense gravity hurled Pioneer 10 toward the edge of the solar system. At one billion miles from the sun, Pioneer 10 passed Saturn. At some two billion miles, it hurtled past Uranus, past Neptune at nearly three billion miles, and past Pluto at almost four billion miles. By 1997, twenty-five years after its launch, Pioneer 10 was more than six billion miles from the sun. Despite that immense distance, Pioneer 10 continued to beam back radio signals to scientists on Earth.

"Perhaps most remarkable," writes Jaroff, "those signals emanate from an eight-watt transmitter, which radiates about as much power as a bedroom night light, and take more than nine hours to reach Earth."

The Little Satellite That Could was not qualified to do what it did. Engineers designed Pioneer 10 with a useful life of just three years. But it kept going and going. By simple longevity, its tiny eight-watt transmitter radio accomplished more than anyone thought possible.[1]

The study of Peter's life parallels Pioneer 10's longevity. Each lesson he learned was a stepping-stone toward his greater usefulness for Christ. Peter reveals his spiritual secret to us toward the end of 1 Peter chapter 1 and continues through the beginning of chapter 2. His rich experience with human failure and spiritual success makes him uniquely qualified to give advice for enduring the race of life.

My most important goal is to finish the race. When I get to heaven, I want to receive my W.D. (Well Done) degree. Sometimes though I get tired, and I am tempted to give in to discouragement. A runner also gets tired especially toward the end of a race. Although he knows the finish line is near, his body is screaming for rest. It is then that he needs to draw on inward reserves for the energy to continue. I have to do the same thing when I'm running on empty. I open my Bible to 1 Peter and discover the faithful steps he took toward his own W.D. degree.

The Precise Perspective

Before my daughter Julie bought her first car, she had a mechanic in our church check it out. She knew that his perspective would be of great help in her decision.

The Lord is the expert on life. When we go to Him and ask for His perspective on our lives, He will show us how He wants us to view this world. "Being born again, not of corruptible seed, but of incorruptible, by the word of God, which liveth and abideth for ever. For all flesh is as grass, and all the glory of man as the flower of grass. The grass withereth, and the flower thereof falleth away: But the word of the Lord endureth for ever. And this is the word which by the gospel is preached unto you" (1 Peter 1:23-25).

No matter how much glory man achieves, he still ages, wrinkles, deteriorates, and finally disappears from the scene. His flesh is no more durable than a piece of grass.

Doris learned this firsthand. She decided to teach in a Christian school in Florida. But she didn't enjoy the small salary and long hours. After a while she decided to quit her job and work somewhere else so she could make more money.

A year later, though, she came back and again applied for a job at the Christian school. The principal asked her why she quit her secular job. She said, "I found out that joy couldn't be bought with a higher salary."

Doris learned that her spiritual joy didn't come from material possessions. She understood that the things of this world will tarnish and decay. She learned to look at this world from a precise godly perspective.

When I travel to India, I often travel light. The national pastors and their families need medicines, clothing, eyeglasses, and church materials. Because of this, I pack a minimum of personal items in order to make the best use of space for their needs. One of my needs is for a disposable razor.

I can't help but reflect on our convenience-loving culture. No one blinks at the thought that a manufacturer has invented a product that is meant to be thrown away after it is used.

When I was growing up, there was a lot more care given to how things were made. A friend told me that his dad went to a department store to buy some new socks. The last time he had bought socks was fifteen years before! Obviously those socks were of good quality!

Yet no matter how much care goes into an item, it will still decay along with everything else in this world. A good friend of mine, Pastor Tom Cucuzza, shared with me that every time he passes a junkyard he thinks, *Every one of those cars was once someone's dream car.*

Realizing the transitory nature of the things of this world is difficult. We hang on to those things, not remembering that they are corruptible. How many times do we think as we drive to work, *This car will be in the junkyard someday. I had better witness to someone, because the human soul is something that will last for eternity.* When the boss suggests a move with an attractive raise, do we think, *I won't move unless I can find a good Bible-believing church in the area.* Or instead, do we think, *This is what I need to move up the career ladder.*

A. W. Tozer once said, "The man who comes to a right belief about God is relieved of ten thousand temporal problems, for he sees at once that these have to do with matters which at the most cannot concern him very long."[2] The apostle Peter knew that believers would be tempted to hold the things of this world in higher esteem than the things of God.

Rosario Pineda Lopez and her family took refuge in her Habitat for Humanity house during Hurricane Mitch when it passed through Nicaragua in August 1999. The home wasn't finished, but it was almost to roof level when the hurricane struck. The family of five fled to the unfinished brick house when floodwaters got waist high in their old house. Lopez learned firsthand that a simple, decent house can be a matter of life and death.[3]

Lopez was fortunate to have such a house to run to in time of trouble, especially in a country where decent housing is rare. But one day even the Lopez family will find out the same thing everyone of us will find out—that a home on this earth, though a great help now, will mean nothing in eternity. It is important that we realize that the structure of hope, the home Christ has for us in heaven, is stronger than any building, home, or residence on this earth.

GRASS 101

Grass is a great thing to compare with our lives on this earth. If the Bible were merely a human book, it would probably compare human life to a mighty oak tree or a towering mountain. But since

God is the author of the Bible, He sees man for what he really is, and consequently He compares man to grass.

All of us should be assigned grass duty once in a while. Sit outside in a patch of yard and study each of the individual blades while considering God's comparison of that lowly plant to your life. Think about how each blade's feeling of superiority vanishes when a lawn mower brings it down to size. Think about the times of drought when the grass dries up, and how we are dependent on God's goodness for satisfaction and fulfillment. Our athletic achievements, financial commitments, and educational advances eventually wither away. Moreover, the final lesson from Grass Duty is that when the individual blade dies, more grass replaces it.

Have you tested your life against the grass? Take a moment, realize that it is only the Word of God that lasts forever, and plan your life accordingly. Perhaps it is time for your neighbor to hear about Christ. Or maybe the local kids would enjoy a basketball game in the park followed by a Bible study. When you consciously decide to put the things of God over the things of this world, you will discover the first part of Peter's secret to spiritual endurance, a precise perspective.

Miraculous Fortitude

We can look back on several millenniums of God's miraculous preservation of His Word and shout with Peter that indeed His Word endures forever!

The Bible, compared with other ancient writings, has more manuscript evidence backing its authenticity than any ten pieces of classical literature combined. A.T. Robertson, the author of the most comprehensive grammar of New Testament Greek, wrote, "There are some 8,000 manuscripts of the Latin Vulgate and at least 1,000 for the other early versions. Add over 4,000 Greek manuscripts, and we have 13,000 manuscript copies of portions of the New

Testament. Besides all this, much of the New Testament can be reproduced from the quotations of the early Christian writers."

The Bible has withstood vicious attacks from its enemies as no other book. Many have tried to burn it, ban it, and outlaw it since the days of the Roman emperors.

Sidney Collett in *All About the Bible* says, "Voltaire, the noted French infidel who died in 1778, said that in 100 years from his time Christianity would be swept from existence and passed into history. But what has happened? Voltaire has passed into history; while the circulation of the Bible continues to increase in almost all parts of the world, carrying blessing wherever it goes." Only fifty years after Voltaire's death, the Geneva Bible Society used his press and house to produce stacks of Bibles.

And these are just a few of the examples of how the mighty hand of God has preserved the Bible down through history.[4]

DON'T GET SIDETRACKED!

Peter explains that the Word of God should be our focus because it endures forever. Since the eternal Scriptures are our reference, it is important in this journey through life that we don't get sidetracked by the trivial.

A family spent a summer traveling around the country. To pass the time, one of the children watched for license plates. The trip to Wyoming netted Larry plates from twenty-four states, and while they were there, he saw four more. The return trip was during peak vacation season, and they went through Yellowstone National Park—a license plate collector's paradise. By the morning of the second day there, he had just one more state to go: Delaware. Larry became obsessed with finding a license plate from Delaware. When they stopped to see Yellowstone's magnificent sights, he didn't glance at them. He preferred to run up and down the parking lots looking at license plates.

The family stopped to eat in a cafeteria near Yellowstone Falls. Larry said, "I don't want to eat. Can't I just stay in the parking lot?"

"No," Mom and Dad said firmly. "You have to eat."

Larry bolted his food and headed back out to the parking lot. When the family came out, Larry came bounding toward them. "Come here! You won't believe it!"

Pulling into a parking space was a blue Volkswagen bus with Delaware license plates. The family took a picture of Larry proudly standing beside the bus. A decade later, when the family looks at their pictures, that one snapshot says more than anything else what they did in Yellowstone.[5]

It is understandable for a young boy to be sidetracked. However, Peter explains that this same thing happens to adult Christians. Peter's call to look at human life as grass will cause you to put aside the inconsequential in the quest for the eternal.

Is your faith a matter of convenience or sacrifice, comfort or surrender? It is only when we fix our eyes on the eternal things of God that we will begin to live in such a way that every thought and every action glorifies Christ. Determine that when you look back at the pictures of your life, you will see more than just trivial pursuits.

An Extraordinary X-ray

My son Jim broke his ankle when he was sixteen. At the hospital an X-ray was taken, and it was determined that the bone required surgery. The X-ray gave the doctors the knowledge they needed to fix the problem.

It is the same way with the Christian life. When we go to the Lord for our eternal glasses, He helps us "X-ray" our lives so we can find the things that are keeping us from enduring.

Peter tells about five dangerous sins that aren't always obvious. These are writhing serpents that blend into their surroundings and thus cause the greatest havoc. And yet God wants us to hold His X-ray up to our lives so we can eradicate those hindrances from our spiritual walk. "Wherefore laying aside all malice, and all guile, and hypocrisies, and envies, and all evil speakings, As newborn babes, desire the sincere milk of the word, that ye may grow thereby: If so be ye have tasted that the Lord is gracious" (1 Peter 2:1-3).

An investigative commission blamed faulty wiring, poor construction, and inadequate supervision for the deadly collapse of a fifty-nine-foot-high pile of logs at Texas A&M University. While preparing the wood for the school's annual bonfire, twelve students died.

The tragedy "has roots in decisions and actions by both students and university officials over many, many years," said Leo Linbeck, a Houston businessman who headed the investigative panel. They "created an environment where a complex and dangerous structure was allowed to be built without controls." The report said that the overall weight of the structure, two million pounds, would have caused problems even with perfect construction.[6]

Even though it should have been obvious to the faculty and staff that a two-million-pound woodpile was a potential hazard, because it was a tradition, they didn't realize the danger. And the same thing can be true for Christians. It is easier to identify the "big" sins such as robbing a bank or having an adulterous affair. Sometimes we think that because we don't do these things, we are "spiritual."

Malice, guile, hypocrisies, envies, and evil speaking—this is quite a list of sins! However, these sins are deep in the soul and therefore more difficult to remove. If they are granted citizenship, they become like the deadly woodpile, ready to cause destruction.

When my children were small, my son's friend swallowed gasoline. We rushed him to the hospital, and the doctors pumped it out of his system. What would you think if on the way to the hospital we had stopped at McDonald's for a hamburger? Obviously, the boy didn't need food! He needed to get his stomach purged of the poison first! Peter explains that the Christian has to deal with these five inward sins before he can desire and receive nourishment from the Word of God.

Malevolent Malice

Years ago I had a man in my church who shared with me that he hadn't spoken to his brother in over fifty years. When I asked him what had happened to cause such a rift, he said that neither one remembered what it was. Unfortunately neither brother asked forgiveness of the other, and as far as I know, they never made up their quarrel.

This standoff might be an extreme example of malice, but the same thing happens even in Christian families and the church. Malice is ill will toward others, and it is more common than any of us care to admit. Some people distill malice like water. It takes a conscious effort to overcome our feelings of resentment when people hurt us. Romans 12:19 states, "Dearly beloved, avenge not yourselves, but rather give place unto wrath: for it is written, Vengeance is mine; I will repay, saith the Lord."

Vengeance belongs only to the Lord, and when we hold on to those hurt feelings, we are taking what belongs to God into our own hands. Malice will keep us in the prison of self-will.

Not long after a wealthy contractor had finished building the Tombs prison in New York, he was found guilty of forgery and sentenced to several years in the prison he had built! As he was escorted into a cell of his own making, the contractor said, "I never dreamed when I built this prison that I would be an inmate one day."[7]

Break out of Vindictive Penitentiary. The key to unlocking the door is letting God handle the vengeance. Once you do this, you will find yourself back on track, finding new excitement in your walk with God.

GUILTY GUILE

When eleven-year-old Melissa Wara received the "Hollywood Squares" handheld electronic game from her grandmother, she was thrilled. Minutes later the girl was back asking her mother, Dianna Wara, a question from the game. "What is *Playboy* magazine?" Stunned, the mother took the game from her daughter and noted a sexually explicit question flashing across the screen. Written clearly across the top of the package were the words, "For Ages 8 & Up." Wara bugged the manufacturer about the game, and they finally agreed to a slight modification. On the label will be the message that parents should consider the fact that the game contains actual questions used on the TV program "Hollywood Squares."[8]

This story provides an example of the next hidden sin. The front of the package said, "For Ages 8 & Up," but the truth was, the game wasn't appropriate for anyone to play. Guile is deceit or craftiness—another huge log added to a precarious woodpile. Planning deceitful schemes, going behind someone's back to push your own agenda, undermining someone in authority—these are all examples of guile. Peter says to beware of this tendency because it is so crafty. We need to examine our own lives and root out the practice of deceiving others.

HIDDEN HYPOCRISY

The number one excuse I have heard through the years for people's failure to come to church is, "Since there are hypocrites in the church, I don't want to come." My answer to that is, since there are hypocrites in every industry and organization in the world, are none of them worthy of joining? The excuse of hypocrisy is a lame one. What people are really saying is, since they are hypocrites themselves, they don't want to add to the number of hypocrites in the church!

However, our walk *must* line up with our talk. I have known some people who are professors of faith rather than possessors. Hypocrisy is masking inward evil by an outward show of righteousness. Hypocrisy is pretending to love another person when we don't. It's pretending to be concerned when we could care less. Hypocrisy affects all of us since it is usually something that only God knows about. It is easy to hide this sin from others.

Take a minute and do some soul-searching. Have you been hypocritical in something you have done lately? Maybe you expect your children to go to Sunday school, but you miss church whenever you feel like it. Or you have made a pledge to read more of the Bible but haven't yet done it on a daily basis. I want to encourage you to be honest with God. If you haven't been doing very well spiritually, then tell Him so. Be honest with Him. He will give you the grace and strength you need. And don't forget, He does forgive!

Unenviable Envy

Envy is another sin often hidden under a cloak of spirituality. Envy is displeasure produced by witnessing or hearing of the prosperity of others. Maybe a man at work got a raise, and instead of being happy for him, you start thinking that you were the one who deserved it. Someone else gets what you perceive as special treatment, and you start feeling sorry for yourself. You forget that God has given you your own blessings and start focusing on what you don't have.

Envy's ugly head reared even in the hearts of James and John just before the arrest and crucifixion of Christ. This is the sin of Cain and of the devil himself. It is the sin that put Jesus on the cross, and yet many times we don't recognize it as a problem. And because we fail to acknowledge it, we continue to manifest its hideous attributes—jealousy and covetousness, allowing Cousin Resentment and Uncle Suspicion free rein as well.

Gainful Gossip

Andrea loved to gossip, but she didn't call it that. Instead she would call her friends and say, "I have an important prayer request to tell you about." And under this guise she would tell the friend a malicious half-truth about another person in the church. One day Andrea went too far. A newcomer left First Church, and the reason soon became apparent. Andrea had repeated an untrue rumor about the visitor. This woman's life was spiritually stymied for some time. It took her awhile to get over Andrea's nasty comments. Maybe we don't think we have this tendency, but Peter says that at all times our words should honor Christ.

I drove past a parking space with a large sign above it. The sign said, "Don't even think about parking here!" And that should be our attitude toward speaking evil of others—don't even think about doing it! Stop your thoughts from going in that direction.

A *National Geographic* article said that Tibetans don't eat fish. Since fish have no tongues, they say they cannot gossip. Since Tibetans consider gossip a cardinal sin, they "reward" fish for their virtue by not eating them. Few things are so attractive as hearing or repeating spicy gossip. Marivaux said, "Some people will believe anything if it is whispered to them." Disparaging chitchat is something everyone admits to be wrong but that, at the same time, almost everyone enjoys. Yet there is nothing so destructive of brotherly love and unity in a family and in a church.

Is There a Cure?

While certain diseases interfere with the process of absorbing food, the spiritual diseases of malice, guile, envy, hypocrisy, and evil-speaking interfere with the absorption of God's Word. Here are some of the reasons:

1) If you are filled with jealousy and slander, you distance yourself from God's people (Mark 11:25).

2) If you hate, you close yourself off to your neighbor and to God (Matthew 5:23-24).

3) If you are a hypocrite, then you can recite the words without any genuine commitment (1 John 3:18).

4) If you are dishonest in your words to others, then the teaching of Scripture will hold little authority over you (Ephesians 4:28).

The Third Step—Craving the Consecrated

Linda and I enjoy eating many different types of foods, but I know that one of her favorites is chocolate. Sometimes when I want to surprise her, I take her to a special place that sells Belgian chocolates. She has told me on more than one occasion, "I crave chocolate."

Peter now writes about a subject dear to his heart—how to crave the consecrated. He told us first about the *nature* of the Word of God, and now he writes of the *nurture* of the Word of God and how best to feed our souls: "As newborn babes, desire the sincere milk of the word, that ye may grow thereby: If so be ye have tasted that the Lord is gracious" (1 Peter 2:2-3).

In a spiritual sense, as we lay aside the old desires, old thoughts, and old ways of our sinful nature, we are to take the positive step of desiring or *craving* pure spiritual milk. The word *desire* is translated from the Greek word *epipotheo*, which means "a strong yearning." This word refers to the deepest desire or longing one can have for something.

In the Antarctic summer of 1908, Sir Ernest Shackleton and three companions attempted to travel to the South Pole from their winter quarters. They set off with four ponies to help carry the load. Six weeks later, their ponies dead and rations all but exhausted, they turned back toward their base, their goal not accomplished. Altogether they trekked 127 days. On the return journey, as Shackleton records in *The Heart of the Antarctic*, the time was spent talking about food—elaborate feasts, gourmet delights, sumptuous menus. As they staggered along, suffering from dysentery, not knowing whether they would survive, every waking hour was occupied with thoughts of eating.

The physical need for food is a great example of what our desire should be for the Word of God. Peter knew that every one of us would be able to understand the need for physical nourishment and can see the implications for our longing for the spiritual.

Some might interpret this verse as Peter calling his readers "baby Christians." And while it is true that new Christians first need to understand what is called the "milk of the Word," or the easier doctrines, before they understand the "meat," or the more complicated doctrines, in a greater sense, Peter is saying that it is important for every believer to have this strong desire for the nourishing milk of the Word of God. He is concerned that they continue to put aside their old sinful nature and desire the Word of God, which will produce a greater level of maturity in them regardless of their starting point. He goes on to explain that if they have tasted that the Lord is good (a quote from Psalm 34:8), then they will want more. The hidden sins of malice and envy are poison, while the Word of God is health and life.

Mr. Smith accompanied his wife on their baby's first visit to the doctor. After thoroughly examining the infant, the doctor prescribed seven steps that would help the baby grow into a healthy adult. That same prescription can be taken into the spiritual realm.

- Daily Food. Take in the pure milk of the Word through study and meditation.
- Fresh Air. Pray often or you will faint. Prayer is the oxygen of the soul.
- Regular Exercise. Put into practice what you learn in God's Word.
- Adequate Rest. Rely on God at all times.

- Clean Surroundings. Avoid those things that weaken you spiritually.
- Loving Care. Be part of a church where you will benefit from a pastor's teaching and Christian fellowship.
- Periodic Checkups. Regularly examine your spiritual health.

Here are some practical ways in which to use the Bible to nourish your soul:

1) Begin reading your Bible fifteen minutes a day. If you are already doing that, read fifteen minutes more (2 Timothy 2:15).

2) Parents, read the Bible to your children before bed or at the dinner table. Make it a focus of family life (Deuteronomy 6:7).

3) Bring your Bible to church and take notes (Deuteronomy 31:12).

4) Listen to the Bible on tape when you are driving or working around the house (Romans 10:17).

5) Replace a half-hour TV show with half an hour of Bible reading (Romans 14:19).

6) Don't be afraid to ask questions about what you are reading (Colossians 3:1).

7) Ask yourself this question: Is it apparent to my family and friends that I love God's Word? (Philippians 3:12).

8) Remember, as James says, when you read the Word, do what it says! (James 1:23-25).

9) A baby isn't afraid to let the whole neighborhood know he is hungry, and we can do no less as Christians. No matter where we are on Righteousness Raceway, we can all learn to intensely crave the Word of God.

One time a preacher met a church member who came to only one service a week. The member said, "Your sermons are so good I can only digest one a week." The preacher said, "I don't think your problem is in digestion; I think your problem is in appetite."

Don't live as a spiritual anorexic. Crave the milk of the Word!

God's Word is not like gum that you chew for a while. It is not junk food. It is nourishing and real. It is meant to be thought about, digested, and acted upon. When you learn to crave the Word of God in this way, you will find yourself wanting more. The desire will come, but you have to discipline yourself first. Don't put off reading the Word of God until you want to do so. Discipline yourself to daily read the Word of God. The love and strong desire to do it will come later. There is no better advice than that. When you train yourself to desire the Word of God, nothing else will satisfy.

Energetic Endurance

What was Peter's spiritual secret? First he had a precise perspective. He saw the things of this world as they really are and the Word of God as the only thing that abides forever. His new spiritual vision enabled him to use the extraordinary X-ray of the Word of God in order to purge malicious hidden sins out of his life. When those sins were gone, he was able to crave what is consecrated. This desire for God's Word gave him renewed spiritual energy, vitality to run the race all the way to the finish line.

Peter's secret is our own. It is only when we follow his pattern that we can begin to understand his perspective. And we can begin to understand his endurance on Righteousness Raceway. He learned to keep his eyes on Christ Jesus.[9] As long as that was his focus, he knew he would stay on track.

Are you losing steam when you ought to be revving up? Fix your eyes on the prize, the high calling of Christ Jesus. Your pace will pick up, your determination will be renewed, and your resolve will strengthen as you learn to let the pure milk of the Word of God nourish your soul.

12

THE GOD OF ALL COMFORT

AS I SPOKE AT OUR Family Camp, I stood on the bank of a beautiful lake in northern Minnesota watching the sun say a brilliant good-bye to the day. A few hundred people sat on benches in front of me. I glanced toward the second row and met the eyes of a church leader. He had been told his wife had an early form of cancer. My gaze wandered to another family, remembering what a miracle it was that they had even come. Their baby had died only six months before. An older gentleman sat on the front row. He was trying to get his life back together after selling his home.

I wanted to share something that would minister to each of their needs, but the needs were so great. How could I be of comfort to them? There were many others who had needs that I wanted to address. I didn't know all the specifics, but I felt the burden of communicating peace to their souls. I glanced down at my open Bible and realized it had opened to a particular passage, Psalm 71.

Instantly my mind transported me back to a time several months before. I was sitting in my living room at two o'clock in the morning. I had suffered severe insomnia for several weeks. Linda was recovering from painful back surgery in the hospital. A dear staff member who was a close friend had left our ministry and the state without telling me why. The pressures of our growing church surrounded me as I sat staring out my living room window. We were in desperate need of a new building, and yet the financial needs of such a project were great.

My Bible lay unopened in my lap. I knew I should pray, and yet when I opened my mouth to try to talk to the Lord, I couldn't form the words. I was tired, physically, mentally, and spiritually. I felt the way I had in the early days of ministry when the crowds fluctuated between five and twenty, and the money was so tight I didn't draw a salary. Except this time there were many more people depending on me for spiritual leadership. But I was weary of leading. I wasn't sure I wanted to continue.

I sat through the long watches of the night. Aimlessly I opened my Bible to the Psalms, thinking that I could identify with David's frustrations. And there it was. A passage that leaped into my consciousness. A chapter that gave me hope for the first time in weeks. I had read this psalm many times before, but never had I comprehended the desolation the psalmist felt. For the first time that night, I began to pray.

"In thee, O LORD, do I put my trust: let me never be put to confusion." [I felt confused. I could identify with the author's feelings!] "Deliver me in thy righteousness, and cause me to escape: [No question about it, I wanted to escape. Hawaii sounded great at the moment!] incline thine ear unto me, and save me." ["Yes, Lord, please listen to me. I'm tired. I'm confused. I'm worried about Linda. I've been betrayed by a close friend. I'm concerned about the finances of the church."]

"Be thou my strong habitation, whereunto I may continually resort: ["Lord, I know You are a strong habitation. I've read in Your Word how You are a strong shield to those who put their trust in You. And yet the pressures are so great that I don't *feel* like trusting You."] thou hast given commandment to save me; for thou art my rock and my fortress." [A fortress is usually built on a hill so that it is hard to attack. The walls are made of stone—hard to penetrate. I knew that a fortress was an analogy of safety in ancient times. "Lord, if You are my fortress, then You are committed to protecting me. You are keeping an eye out for those who wish to attack me."]

"Deliver me, O my God, out of the hand of the wicked, out of the hand of the unrighteous and cruel man." ["Although I know there are many people who support me and love me, now I feel as if everyone is out to get me. And yet my hope is in You, Lord."]

"For thou art my hope, O Lord GOD: thou art my trust from my youth." ["Lord, You are my hope!" I had just finished studying the life of the apostle Peter. I saw that he also knew this truth. "Even after he denied You, You said, 'Tell the disciples and Peter.' You didn't leave Peter out! And later You gave him authority to nurture the flock of God. How honored he must have felt. In spite of his failure, he lived in hope because of Your forgiveness and love!"]

"By thee have I been holden up from the womb: thou art he that took me out of my mother's bowels: my praise shall be continually of thee. I am as a wonder unto many; but thou art my strong refuge." ["I praise You, Lord, for being my refuge."]

"Let my mouth be filled with thy praise and with thy honour all the day." ["Lord, I do wish to praise You! But I still feel the burden of my problems."] "Cast me not off in the time of old age; forsake me not when my strength faileth." ["I need Your strength because my strength has failed!"]

"For mine enemies speak against me; and they that lay wait for my soul take counsel together, saying, God hath forsaken him: persecute and take him; for there is none to deliver him." ["Lord, I know this is true of me at this moment; there are those who don't want me to continue. I know You are in control. This has been the longest night of my life, and yet, Lord, from this window I can see the sun starting to light up the sky. I needed this reminder that You are the light of my life."]

"O God, be not far from me: O my God, make haste for my help." ["Lord, You *have* helped me. You *have* strengthened me. I know there will be more difficulties ahead, but I know You are there, and You will continue to give me the energy I need to continue."]

"Let them be confounded and consumed that are adversaries to my soul; let them be covered with reproach and dishonour that seek my hurt. But I will hope continually, and will yet praise thee more and more." ["My hope is in You! Just as Peter knew this, so once again am I reminded that You are there for me. You are the reason I have hope."]

"My mouth shall shew forth thy righteousness and thy salvation all the day; for I know not the numbers thereof. I will go in the strength of the Lord GOD: I will make mention of thy righteousness, even of thine only." ["Help me to encourage others when they are facing difficult times, Lord."]

"O God, thou hast taught me from my youth: and hitherto have I declared thy wondrous works. Now also when I am old and greyheaded, O God, forsake me not; until I have shewed thy strength unto this generation, and thy power to every one that is to come. Thy righteousness also, O God, is very high, who hast done great things: O God, who is like unto thee! Thou, which hast shewed me great and sore troubles, shalt quicken me again, and shalt bring me up again from the depths of the earth." ["I feel like I have come up from the depths of the earth, Lord. You have brought me here. Even though I know my problems won't be solved overnight, I praise You for being in charge and working everything out for my good."]

"Thou shalt increase my greatness, and comfort me on every side. I will also praise thee with the psaltery, even thy truth, O my God: unto thee will I sing with the harp, O thou Holy One of Israel. My lips shall greatly rejoice when I sing unto thee; ["I am not known for my singing abilities, but if I sing to You, I'm sure You will appreciate it at least!"] and my soul, which thou hast redeemed. My tongue also shall talk of thy righteousness all the day long: for they are confounded, for they are brought unto shame, that seek my hurt" (Psalm 71:1-24).

Perhaps God gave me this comfort in the past so I could meet the needs of the people who sat in front of me. I realized this was the perfect psalm to address the needs of the congregation. I read it with passion and fervor, but at times my voice broke as I remembered my brokenness of spirit during my all-night vigil. I shared how the Lord had brought me comfort. I admitted that my problems didn't go away instantly, but I saw God work in my life. I explained that my Bible is the most worn in the Psalms because that was where I lived for so many months. And I explained that I knew now more than ever that only God can bring comfort to our deepest level of pain.

After the service many families came to me and said what a blessing my message was to them. Others came forward and asked for special prayer, sharing with me some of the struggles they were facing.

Then I saw them. Two eight-year-old boys at the back of the group. Their cocky smiles made me a bit nervous. I wondered what they wanted to say. They waited for everyone to finish talking to me. Then they strode forward. One boy said, "Pastor, we heard you say that your Bible was the most worn in the Psalms, and we want to see your Bible." I felt relieved. No problem there.

I gave them my Bible. One of the boys opened it to the middle, and I saw him turn page by page until he got to the Psalms. Each page was worn, and many passages were underlined. Sometimes the writing was blurred where tears had fallen. Satisfied, the boys handed the Bible back. "You did live in the Psalms, preacher. We can tell."

A Lesson for Life

I've shared many instances of Peter's humanness and God's grace in times of stress. Remembering those occurrences in Peter's life have brought me comfort, and I hope they have given you help as well. Peter experienced spiritual success because he learned from his failures. And spiritual success should be every Christian's goal. Biblical success is different from the success you'd hear about in a business seminar.

- Success is not wealth.
- Success is not numbers.
- Success is not outward appearance.
- Success is not health.
- Success is not impressing others.
- Success is not having an easy path.

A word that captures the biblical idea of success for the Christian is *growth*. Looking at every event—whether disastrous, difficult, or delightful—as a stepping-stone toward spiritual growth provides a godly perspective. Romans 8:28 states, "And we know that all things work together for good to them that love God, to them who are the called according to his purpose." The words "all things" encompass every aspect of our lives, even our failures. When we love God and serve Him, then He works all events in our lives ultimately for His purpose.

Success Is Not Wealth

God makes no distinction in the Bible between those who were blessed with wealth and those who weren't. Abraham had vast herds and hundreds of servants, and yet Christ had no place to lay His head. Job was the wealthiest man in his area; then he lost it all. But in the trials he faced, it is clear he wasn't successful in God's eyes because of his wealth. Part of his success was due to his lack of attachment to his wealth.

The apostle Paul knew how to abound and how to be abased (Philippians 4:12). In Bible college one of my teachers, Dr. Mark Cambron, commented on Paul's attitude. He said that if Paul was invited to a believer's home and was offered T-bone steak, he would say, "Brother, bless you for having such a wonderful dinner! I would enjoy eating steak with you!" On the other hand if a less wealthy believer said, "Brother Paul, we would like you to come over, but all we are having is rice," Paul would say, "I love rice! It will be wonderful to fellowship with your family."

Paul understood one of the secrets to the Christian life—contentment. And that is why even though some of God's choicest servants lived and died in poverty (Hebrews 11:37), they understood that success can't be measured by abundance.

Success Is Not Numbers

Peter won multitudes at Pentecost. Jeremiah had few if any followers. Noah preached for 120 years but won only his own wife and children. Thousands followed Christ for bread and healing but deserted Him in Jerusalem. Paul won few in Thessalonica but many in Berea with the same message. Numbers—whether it be church members, wins and losses, or annual sales figures—are sometimes affected by factors beyond our control. People today don't want to admit they're not always in control. However, this desire to control is a failure to submit to God's will. Noah is commended (Hebrews 11:7; 2 Peter 2:5) though the "First Baptist Church of Mt. Ararat" had only eight members. Jeremiah and Paul didn't seem to worry that their success couldn't be tangibly counted.

Success Is Not Outward Appearance

Saul looked like a king. He literally stood head and shoulders above every other man in the country. But he was a failure as a monarch because of his character flaws. David did not have a regal appearance. He was young and small. But despite a blatant failure in his own life, he was Israel's greatest king.

This fixation on the superficial characterizes our culture today. America at the beginning of the twenty-first century is obsessed with the outward appearance. We spend billions trying to improve the outer shell and drive many of our young people to bulimia and anorexia in their attempt to have an "acceptable" body.

An author came across a fax summary of news and commentary from the *New York Times*. It said that Stanford University's faculty had just voted overwhelmingly to tighten a lax grading system under which hardly any student flunked a class and nearly everyone received A's and B's almost as a matter of entitlement. The article went on to say that the failing grade would be restored, and teachers would be encouraged to award C's and D's when deserved. It seems that those two letters had virtually disappeared from the dazzling but misleading transcripts that a generation of Stanford students (and those at plenty of other places) had used to impress parents, employers, and graduate school deans.

The article ended with this piercing indictment. "The sad truth is that Stanford's permissive practices were merely the final expression of a sensibility that seeks to eliminate the *fear of failure*, holds that *feeling good* is more important than doing well and assumes that somehow students can be injected with self-esteem rather than earning it by honest toil."[1] Success has to be measured by the effort put into it. It cannot be dependent on outward appearance.

SUCCESS IS NOT HEALTH

"If you've got your health, you've got everything" goes an old saying; that's absolutely untrue. There are many things more important than health. Many of the greatest men and women of history have had to endure weak constitutions, ill health, and disabilities. Three times Paul asked the Lord to remove his "thorn in the flesh," and three times his request was refused. This thorn is not described in Scripture, and I think the reason is so that none of us can judge and say, "Paul suffered that, but what I suffer is much worse." Paul's answer from God is the one suffering Christians have believed for centuries: "My grace is sufficient for you." Sometimes it is necessary to suffer from physical ailments in order to have spiritual success.

Success Is Not Impressing Others

The Greek word for "witness" also gives us the English word *martyr*. In the early church witnessing for Christ often ended in martyrdom, so a new word was coined. Peter told the Sanhedrin in no uncertain terms that he and the other apostles were far more concerned with pleasing God than with pleasing man. Christ told us to beware of the time when all men would speak well of us.[2]

Success Is Not Having an Easy Path

Some believers have misconceptions about difficulties in a Christian's life. First, they often think that once a person is saved, God will smooth all the bumps in the road, and life will be a bed of roses. Second, they assume that if a Christian's life is hard, God must be punishing him. While it is true that suffering is sometimes chastisement from the Lord, it is also true that affliction is part of the Christian life. The Bible commands us to "endure hardness." Without suffering, we would never have the Psalms. I would never have gleaned the comfort from Psalm 71 if the psalmist had never endured adversity. The author of Hebrews said we are more than conquerors *in* trials (Hebrews 11:35b-38).

Judging Spiritual Success

If outward appearance, health, and wealth are not elements of spiritual accomplishment, then by what standards do we measure success? It is God, the Author of the Bible, to whom we are accountable. It is Christ before whom we will ultimately stand. He will ultimately determine our success or failure. The Judgment Seat of Christ is where the believer will be judged for his works. This is a judgment of believers for rewards or lack of rewards. No unbelievers are judged at this time.

The Bible also speaks of the Great White Throne Judgment

(Revelation 20:12-15) where unbelievers are judged for their unbelief and cast into hell. This is an entirely different judgment that happens at a separate time with a different group of people.

Second Corinthians 5:10 explains, "For we must all appear before the judgment seat of Christ; that every one may receive the things done in his body, according to that he hath done, whether it be good or bad." We will be judged for what we have done for Christ (not for what we own or look like or what people thought of us) to see if it was good or bad. Matthew 25:14-30 gives insight into how the believer will be judged. The stewards in this parable are judged according to their faithfulness in discharging their duty.

Success involves pursuing godliness by being conformed to Christ, a goal we can't achieve on our own. We need to let the Holy Spirit guide our every thought in order to accomplish this. Successful living comes from adhering to biblical principles in spite of trial, hardship, and temptation. Ultimate success is hearing Christ say, "Well done," and being crowned at the Judgment Seat.

When Peter appears before the Judgment Seat of Christ, he won't fear. Because of his faithful obedience to the Lord, he will hear, "Well done," from his Lord. Each trial in his life was a lesson learned in obedience to God. Each lesson realized from his failures served to make him stronger.

Let's look briefly at each lesson Peter learned in his journey toward spiritual success.

SUCCESS IS SYNONYMOUS WITH SERVICE

Peter saw Christ minister to each disciple in numerous ways before His crucifixion. However, when Jesus washed the disciples' feet, Peter learned that in the deepest sorrow, it is essential to be in the deepest service.

God Doesn't Fit in a Box

In the upper room Peter said he would follow the Lord wherever He led. Yet an indescribable barrier rose up in Peter's path. Why couldn't he follow the Lord? Because he *thought* he could. Christians might admit their own failures and inadequacies, but there is a difference between saying we fail and having a deep sense of our own helplessness and our dependence on the Lord. Peter was walking by sight rather than by faith, and it took the trial and crucifixion of Jesus for him to understand this.

Peter was a determined person, and such people often find it hard to renounce their self-confidence. We do not reach the life of real faith until we are fully conscious of our own helplessness. How can we trust Christ unless we have thoroughly learned to distrust ourselves?

As long as Peter saw Christ performing miracles or being greeted by hosannas, it was easy to follow, but when the crowds turned on Him, Peter's courage forsook him. It is not by saying, "I will follow You, Lord," that we succeed in following Him. It is by bringing our hearts into full harmony with His divine will.[3]

Peter learned that instead of making his own plans and asking God to bless them, he was a cog in the wheel of God's plan. He learned to relinquish his own pride and found that grace is a humbling truth. Grace leaves no place for pride because only God gives this gift. Grace insists that we are utterly worthless and helpless, and our only hope lies outside ourselves in Christ. Grace and pride are absolute strangers to each other.[4]

Peter's parting admonition is, "But grow in grace, and in the knowledge of our Lord and Saviour Jesus Christ. To him be glory both now and for ever. Amen" (2 Peter 3:18). Peter found out that growing in grace came from yielding first to His will.

THE GOD OF THE EVERYDAY

Peter saw how Christ handled the pressure of Judas' betrayal. He learned how to cope especially when the pressures of life threatened to boil over. Peter learned to look toward his hope of heaven. And that is what the believer needs to do. One writer said that hope is taking hold of the future. That act prevents us from giving undue attention to what is only present and temporal.[5] Peter learned how to depend on God's strength.

Many years ago a group of campers sat around a campfire. One friend challenged another by saying he could place a paper cup in the middle of the fire and guarantee that it would not burn. Someone offered him a Coke if he could do it. The boy took a paper cup, filled it with water, and placed it in the middle of the fire. The heat curled the edge of the cup over to the water line, but the cup did not burn. Then the boy reached into the fire, grabbed the cup, emptied out the water, and threw the cup back into the flames. The cup burned instantly.

The Holy Spirit is the water in our lives that keeps us from burning up from the pressures around us. As long as we lean on His strength, we will be protected.

WHEN FAILURE IS A RESULT OF SIN

J. Hudson Taylor once said, "I have failed . . . I am failing . . . I will fail . . . but Jesus never fails." Our hope is not in our ability to stand, but in *His ability* to protect and sustain us.

Without failure we can't expect to learn. The only way a high-jumper can discover his limit is to jump until he misses. That's why Bill Gates, former CEO of Microsoft, says, "Success is a terrible teacher." When we are succeeding, we tend to focus on things that aren't essential, but failure has a way of getting our attention! The way to overcome *fear* of failure is to remove the *sting* of failure. Failure can't hurt you if you learn from it. It can only help you.[6]

The apostle Paul said, "When I am weak, then I am strong." This is the paradox of the Christian life. When we are the most dependent on Christ, we are in the least danger. In those times when we feel so ill-equipped and "needy," we are the strongest—because we have stopped relying on our own strength and devices and instead are resting in Him.

When Your Dreams Shatter

Peter learned to look to God's plans for his life rather than rely on his own dreams. He found that Christ's will for Him was greater than anything he could have imagined for himself. Here is a short list of what he accomplished:

- He stood up and preached to thousands on the day of Pentecost. (Acts 2:14)
- He refused to be bullied into silence by the civil leaders and instead responded, "We must obey God rather than men." (Acts 5:29)
- He was thrown in jail for his faith, but he would not recant. (Acts 12:4-5)
- He was the on the forefront of erasing the barrier between Jewish and Gentile Christians. (Acts 10)
- He was a prominent spokesman in the early church. (Acts 8:14)
- He wrote two books of the Bible.
- Tradition says he was martyred in Rome. It also states that Peter was crucified upside down because he did not feel worthy to be crucified in the same manner as his Lord.

Using the Past as a Tool for Good

Peter urged us in his epistle to remember what God had done in the past. Looking at the times when God was with us even in deepest sorrow can strengthen us for the future.

Also suffering hardship makes people more sympathetic toward others. A pastor will be limited in effectiveness in the times of sadness until he has been there himself. In suffering people learn compassion. In failure people learn about mercy. Through their sin they come to understand grace.[7]

Holy in an Unholy World

Through the crucible of suffering, Peter learned that holiness was a day-to-day, moment-by-moment decision. A doctor once told a famous preacher that health is not something that can be produced or made by medicine or surgery. Rather, many factors contribute to health—among them genetics, diet, and exercise.

The same principle can be applied to holiness. Special rituals do not make the believer holy. Rather it is a daily diet of the Word of God, prayer, and witnessing to others of our faith that leads to growth. It is what we do rather than what we don't do that brings holiness.[8]

Motivating Fear

Looking at the fatherhood of God, Peter explains a precious truth. Instead of using your earthly father as an example, look first to God. He is the ultimate Father, and His love for you is unconditional. Peter then tells us how the fear of God along with the hope of God balances us in our holiness quest.

Purity Brings Love

Peter knew that purity was essential, and he explains that pushing toward it motivates us to love others.

Tree-skiing may sound like a death wish, but some skiers love the risk of skiing virgin powder lying in a stand of aspen or spruce. The key, of course, is to avoid hitting the trees! In *Outside* magazine, writer and skier Tim Etchells lays out the challenge: "Even more so than in deep snow or moguls, what you focus your eyes on becomes critical in the woods. Look at the spaces between the trees—the exits where you hope to be traveling. As extreme-skiing world champion Kim Reichelm said, 'Don't stare at what you don't want to hit.'"[9]

When the believer pushes for purity, he will focus not on the obstacles but on loving others.

How to Endure

Driving a car is a good example of the need to deal appropriately with the reality of the present. Driving down the road at sixty miles per hour requires us to look forward and focus ahead. Reality is what we see approaching us. We must be able to deal with what we see through the windshield in order to survive.

Drivers need to maintain perspective and know what is approaching from the rear. For that purpose a small rearview mirror is attached to the windshield of the car. It is small in comparison to the windshield because it is of much less importance. Yet without it we could easily be run over by a semi before knowing anything was following too closely. It helps us stay ahead of disaster. The rearview mirror is essential for safe driving.

So the believer needs to look forward for God's direction, all the while watching for potential dangers that could zap his spiritual progress. Peter shares this lesson from personal experience.

Overcoming Failure

Here are five steps toward overcoming your own failures. Just as Peter, Paul, Jeremiah, Noah, and every other great man and woman in the Bible failed, you will experience times of discouragement. It might be because of your own sin or because of circumstances beyond your control. You could feel like a failure because your life hasn't turned out the way you thought it should. Whatever the reason, there is a biblical solution.

Step 1—Admit/Accept Failure

If sin is the reason for failure, then we need to *admit it* and confess it. If sin is not the cause, then we have to *accept* the failure. Don't be afraid to acknowledge the position you are in. No matter what you have done, you are not hopelessly lost from God's grace.

The first step to being right with God is to admit the condition of your soul. Jesus didn't pay for your sins because you were good. It was when you were dead in sins that He died for you. He didn't come to those who were spiritually well; He came to those who were sick, hurting, and troubled (Mark 2:17). Accept His forgiveness today (1 John 1:9).

Step 2—Realize That Your Status in God's Eyes Hasn't Changed

Understand that failure does not change your value as a human being because your value is determined by the love of God, which is unchanging (John 5:24). When we go to God, we don't give Him our resumés and hope He will "hire" us. He will use us right where we are, once we have restored fellowship with Him.

Step 3—Think Realistically

Look at your failure in the light of eternity. Will the loss of my business, job, health, wealth, dreams, etc., matter in eternity? Ask yourself if the failure is a lesson from God and whether you will be better off in eternity because of your failure (1 Peter 2:19).

Step 4—Make Holiness a Habit

Maintain your spiritual discipline. Don't fall asleep on your watch. Reread the suggestions in chapter 8 and chapter 11. Renew your commitment to holy living.

Step 5—Don't Let Embarrassment Keep You from Church and Godly Friends

In times of failure, deal with the problem quickly. Don't wander away from the church in embarrassment. Confess your sin to the Lord if you have sinned against Him. And if you need to, confess to any others you might have wronged. But don't stay away from church and godly friends when you fail. You need them for accountability and support. They will be your lifeline in helping you stay strong.

Hope in Heaven

A preacher told me a story that had changed his perception of heaven. A young boy was orphaned at an early age. He wondered what was to become of him. An aunt he had never met volunteered to take him in.

It was very late at night when a couple from a neighboring farm brought him to her house. He didn't even know if she would be awake. But as they pulled into the yard, there was a candle lit in the window. Its welcome glow warmed the boy's sorrowful heart.

This aunt raised him and provided for him, giving him a secure Christian home. If it was possible, he loved her more than a boy could love his own mother. He understood more than most the anguish of loss, and so this new mother in his life brought him great joy. The boy grew up to become a famous preacher and missionary.

Years later the aunt lay dying. In those long hours in bed, she began to wonder if her life had any significance. She no longer was able to give to others as she had in the past, and the ache in her heart was great. She wrote a letter explaining this to her adopted son. The letter she received from him brought untold joy:

> Dear Aunt,
> You are about to embark on the greatest journey of all. As soon as you close your eyes, you will open them to a light even greater than the candle I first saw when I came to your house so many years ago. The Lord Jesus is waiting up for you just as you waited up for me. He will be your light. You can rest knowing that your life was worthwhile, for as you pointed me to the Lord Jesus, so I have pointed others to the light of the world. Auntie, you're expected! I know. I once saw God standing in your doorway long ago!

Just as the faithful aunt didn't receive her true reward until heaven, so the Christian's reward for enduring adversity won't come until later. We will stand at the Judgment Seat of Christ and be judged right along with Peter. It will be a perfect judgment such as no man on earth could attempt. And it will make every sorrow, injustice, and bitterness we have drunk from the cup of life worth it all.

The Sweet Is in the Bitter

Martin Luther said, "If we consider the greatness and the glory of the life we shall have, it would not be difficult at all for us to bear the concerns of this world." Another author wrote, "True success involves seeking God, loving God, considering God in everything, serving God in everything, and making every aspect of our lives holy by doing everything in His name and for His glory."[10]

At the end of his life, when Peter looked in the mirror, he saw not himself but Christ. He saw not his own failures, but Jesus' righteousness. He saw not his own successes but Christ's blood. He saw his life the way we should see ours.

Will you look into the mirror with the Lord? Will you place your sorrows and hardships into His hand? When you do this, you will see what it means to be successful in God's eyes. You will adopt as your life verse Peter's parting admonition, "But grow in grace, and in the knowledge of our Lord and Saviour Jesus Christ" (2 Peter 3:18a).

You will learn as he did that failure is not permanent, but it can be productive—that it is inevitable and invaluable. Peter recognized that learning from failure equaled success.

I extend to you an invitation to discover God's grace in the midst of trials, failures, and hardships. His grace will guide you through every challenging obstacle. In my deepest despair, He renewed my soul, and I know He will restore you to faith and hope in *your* journey toward success.

Appendix

How to Know for Sure You Are Going to Heaven

Realize first that everyone is less perfect than a holy God. We are all sinners and unable to save ourselves.

"For all have sinned, and come short of the glory of God" (Romans 3:23).

God says that even our good deeds are unclean in his sight. Our good deeds can never pay the price for our sin.

"But we are all as an unclean thing, and all our righteousnesses are as filthy rags; and we all do fade as a leaf; and our iniquities, like the wind, have taken us away" (Isaiah 64:6).

The result and penalty of sin is death, which means separation from God forever.

"For the wages of sin is death; but the gift of God is eternal life through Jesus Christ our Lord" (Romans 6:23).

Because we have sinned, we all deserve to be separated from God forever. God hates sin because it separates us from Him, but He loves us, the sinners.

Heaven is a perfect place; therefore, no sin can enter there. Man must be perfect to gain entrance.

"And there shall in no wise enter into it any thing that defileth, neither whatsoever worketh abomination, or maketh a lie: but they which are written in the Lamb's book of life" (Revelation 21:27).

NOTHING MAN CAN DO COULD HELP OBTAIN THE PERFECTION GOD REQUIRES FOR HEAVEN.

"For by grace are ye saved through faith; and that not of yourselves: it is the gift of God: Not of works, lest any man should boast" (Ephesians 2:8-9).

Salvation is only by God's grace. Grace means unmerited favor or undeserved mercy. A gift is not earned or paid for, or it would not be a gift.

"But to him that worketh not, but believeth on him that justifieth the ungodly, his faith is counted for righteousness" (Romans 4:5).

CHRIST MADE A COMPLETE PAYMENT FOR ALL SIN AND OFFERS HIS RIGHTEOUSNESS TO US.

"For he hath made him to be sin for us, who knew no sin; that we might be made the righteousness of God in him" (2 Corinthians 5:21).

We have seen that we are all sinners and that the penalty of sin is eternal separation from God. We have also seen that God loves us and offers us the gift of eternal life. He requires only our belief, our trust in His payment for our sins.

How could a holy God give eternal life to sinners? Only through His Son who died on the cross to make a full payment for all sin.

ALL WE HAVE TO DO TO HAVE ETERNAL LIFE IS BELIEVE IN JESUS CHRIST.

"For God so loved the world, that he gave his only begotten Son, that whosoever believeth in him should not perish, but have everlasting life" (John 3:16).

This verse does not say anything about promising God good works in order to be saved. It doesn't mention joining a church or being baptized or never committing another sin. The word *believe* means to trust, depend, or rely upon.

Will you place your trust in Jesus Christ to save your soul? To trust Him means to rely totally on Him, not on your own good works. Will you do this right now?

IF YOU HAVE TRUSTED JESUS CHRIST AS YOUR SAVIOR, THEN YOU CAN KNOW YOU HAVE ETERNAL LIFE. GOD HAS PROMISED THIS IN HIS WORD.

"These things have I written unto you that believe on the name of the Son of God; that ye may *know* that ye have eternal life, and that ye may believe on the name of the Son of God" (1 John 5:13).

For more information contact:

Quentin Road Ministries
60 Quentin Road
Lake Zurich, IL 60047
1-800-78GRACE
www.qrm.org

NOTES

CHAPTER 1
EVEN THE BEST FAIL

1. Kent and Barbara Hughes, *Liberating Ministry from the Success Syndrome* (Wheaton, Ill.: Tyndale, 1988), p. 9.
2. Warren Wiersbe, *On Being a Servant of God* (Grand Rapids: Baker Books, 1993), p. 126.
3. Norman Vincent Peale, *The Power of Positive Thinking* (Pawling, N.Y.: Foundation for Christian Living, 1978), p. 126.
4. Robert Tuck, *A Homiletic Commentary on the General Epistles of I and II Peter, I, II, and III John, Jude and the Revelation of St. John the Divine* (New York and London: Funk and Wagnall's Company), p. 2.
5. M. R. DeHaan, *Simon Peter, Sinner and Saint* (Grand Rapids: Zondervan, 1954), p. 29.
6. J. C. Ryle, *Expository Thoughts on the Gospels, Matthew* (Grand Rapids: Zondervan), p. 199.

CHAPTER 2
THE TOWEL, THE WAY TO THE THRONE

1. Steve May, *Ministry Now*, ministrynow.com, May 2000.
2. C. K. Barrett, *The Gospel According to St. John* (London: S.P.C.K., 1975), p. 366-367.
3. 1 Peter 5:7.
4. *Today in the Word*, Moody Bible Institute, March 6, 1991.
5. Kent and Barbara Hughes, *Liberating Ministry from the Success Syndrome* (Wheaton, Ill.: Tyndale, 1987), p. 48-49.
6. Ibid., p. 49.
7. M. R. DeHaan, *Simon Peter, Sinner and Saint* (Grand Rapids: Zondervan, 1954), p. 148.
8. Charles Simpson, *Pastoral Renewal*, December 1998.

CHAPTER 3
PETER SAYS THE WRONG THING THE RIGHT WAY

1. Viola Walden, *Under Construction, Pardon the Mess* (Murfreesboro, Tenn.: Sword of the Lord Publishers, 1994), p. 23.
2. Ephesians 4:29.

3. Woodrow Kroll, *7 Secrets to Spiritual Success* (Sisters, Ore.: Multnomah Publishers, 2000), p. 51.
4. J. C. Ryle, *Ryle's Expository Thoughts on the Gospels, Matthew* (Grand Rapids: Zondervan), p. 312.
5. Jeremiah 29:11.
6. Charles Stanley, *How to Handle Adversity* (Nashville: Thomas Nelson Publishers, 1973), p. 39.
7. Jeremiah 17:9.
8. A. W. Tozer, *The Pursuit of God* (Wheaton, Ill.: Tyndale, n.d.), p. 103.

CHAPTER 4
HOW TO COPE IN THE PRESSURE COOKER

1. 2 Peter 1:4.
2. Mark 10:37.
3. Matthew 16:16.
4. James M. Freeman, *The New Manners and Customs of the Bible* (New Brunswick, N.J.: Bridge-Logos Publishers, 1998), p. 471.
5. Eugene Petersen, "Success or Failure," *Leadership Journal,* 4, Winter 1984, p. 53.
6. J. C. Ryle, *Ryle's Expository Thoughts on the Gospels, Mark* (Grand Rapids: Zondervan), p. 313.

CHAPTER 5
HOW COULD A CHRISTIAN DO *THAT?*

1. Rob Gilbert, *Bits and Pieces*, March 2000, p. 9-11.
2. John Maxwell, *Failing Forward* (Nashville: Thomas Nelson Publishers, 2000), p. 116-117.
3. "They Shoot Christians, Don't They?" Diane Kippers, *Christianity Today*, July 20, 1992, p. 35.
4. G. Campbell Morgan, "The Sifting of Peter," a sermon delivered in 1903 and archived on www.txdirect.net/tgarner/morgan.
5. Matthew 16:18.
6. M. R. DeHaan, *Simon Peter, Sinner and Saint* (Grand Rapids: Zondervan, 1954), p. 67.
7. Luke 24:12.
8. Jonathan Edwards, *Jonathan Edwards on Knowing Christ* (Edinburgh: The Banner of Truth Trust, 1990), p. 164.
9. Leroy Eims, *The Lost Art of Disciple Making* (Grand Rapids: Zondervan, 1978), p. 53.
10. Warren Wiersbe, *On Being a Servant of God* (Grand Rapids: Baker Books, 1993), p. 108.

11. Marla Donato, "Firefighter Hero Is Hurt in South Side Fire," *Chicago Tribune*, Internet Edition, March 24, 2000.
12. *Christian Values Qs Quarterly*, Spring/Summer 1994, p. 10.
13. Luke 17:45; Mark 9:12; Mark 8:31.

CHAPTER 6
HOPE EVEN WHEN IT'S HOPELESS

1. D. Martyn Lloyd-Jones (1898-1981), "A Living Hope of the Hereafter," www.txdirect.net/tgarner/lloydjones2.
2. Philippians 1:6.
3. Warren Wiersbe, *Be Hopeful* (Colorado Springs: Chariot Victor Publishing, 1982), p. 21.
4. Deborah Hastings, *The Associated Press*, March 28, 1997.
5. Rick McGinnis, "A Reason to Hope," 1997, 3-7, www.northheartland.org.
6. *Our Daily Bread*, RBC Ministries, May 7, 1992.

CHAPTER 7
LOOKING BACKWARD TO LOOK FORWARD

1. Rob Gilbert, *Bits and Pieces,* July 1991, p. 5-7.
2. Mark 16:7.
3. John Maxwell, *Injoy Life Club*, April 6, 1993.
4. David Roper, *Tried by Fire* (Palo Alto: Discovery Publishing, 1995), p. 6-8.
5. Job 2:9.
6. Tim Kimmel, *Little House on the Freeway* (Sisters, Ore.: Multnomah Publishers, 1994), p. 106-107.
7. Kent and Barbara Hughes, *Liberating Ministry from the Success Syndrome* (Wheaton, Ill.: Tyndale, 1988), p. 153.
8. Roper, *Tried by Fire*, p. 6-8.

CHAPTER 8
HOLINESS IS NOT WHAT YOU THINK IT IS

1. Tim Kimmel, *Little House on the Freeway* (Sisters, Ore.: Multnomah Publishers, 1994), p. 131.
2. Peter H. Davids, *The First Epistle of Peter* (Grand Rapids: Eerdmans, 1990), p. 66.
3. Hebrews 12:1.
4. Dictionary entry: *legalism* in *Random House Webster's College Dictionary* (New York: Random House, 1999).
5. Biblical Studies Foundation, www.bible.org/docs/nt/books/1pe/deffin/1pet-06.htm., 1997.

6. Ron Ritchie, *What Should Be an Alien in the Midst of Suffering?* (Palo Alto: Discovery Publishing, 1996).

Chapter 9
How Peter Overcame His Inferiority

1. Rob Gilbert, *Bits and Pieces*, October 1992, p. 13.
2. Joel Steven Rouse, "Diving In," www.olympic-usa.org/sports_az/dv/041700feature.html, April 30, 2000.
3. *Today in the Word*, Moody Bible Institute, August 8, 1992.

Chapter 10
How to Be Purified When You Are Petrified

1. B. C. Collin, *First Peter*, "The Pulpit Commentary," ed. H. D. M. Spence and Joseph S. Exell (Grand Rapids: Eerdmans, 1950), p. 11.
2. Rob Gilbert, *Bits and Pieces,* April 2000, p. 12.
3. Jon Johnston, *You Can Stand Strong in the Face of Fear* (Colorado Springs, Colo.: Scripture Press Publications, 1990), p. 111-113.

Chapter 11
Peter's Spiritual Secret

1. Leon Jaroff, "Still Ticking," *Time*, November 4, 1996, p. 80, as quoted by Craig Brian Larson in *Pastoral Grit: The Strength to Stand and to Stay* (Minneapolis: Bethany House Publishers, 1998), pp. 53-54.
2. Tim Hansel, *Eating Problems for Breakfast* (Dallas: Word Publishing, 1988), p. 33.
3. Chris Little, Megan Bieritz, www.habitat.org/intl/mitch/rebuilding, August/September 1999.
4. Josh McDowell, *Evidence That Demands a Verdict* (San Bernardino, Calif.: Campus Crusade for Christ, 1972), p. 21-23.
5. *Signs of the Times*, Moody Bible Institute, August 1992, p. 12.
6. "Playing with Fire," *World*, May 13, 2000, p. 10.
7. *Today in the Word*, Moody Bible Institute, July 12, 1993.
8. Michael D'Antonio, "They Call This a Toy?!" *Good Housekeeping*, June 2000, p. 84.
9. Philippians 3:14.

Chapter 12
The God of All Comfort

1. Gary J. Oliver, *How to Get It Right After You've Gotten It Wrong* (Wheaton, Ill.: Victor Books, 1995), p. 182.
2. Luke 6:26.

3. Joseph S. Exell, *The Biblical Illustrator, John (*Grand Rapids: Baker Book House), p. 453-454.
4. M. R. DeHaan, *Simon Peter, Sinner and Saint* (Grand Rapids: Zondervan, 1954), p. 128-129.
5. Robert Tuck, *A Homiletic Commentary on the General Epistles of I and II Peter, I, II, III John, Jude, and Revelation of St. John the Divine* (New York: Funk and Wagnall's Company), p. 20-22.
6. Steve May, *Ministry Now,* ministrynow.com, November 1999.
7. Bruce Goettsche, www.unionchurch.com/archive/042097.html, April 20, 1997.
8. D. M. Lloyd-Jones, *Expository Sermons on 2 Peter* (Bath, England: The Banner of Truth Trust, 1999), p. 235-237.
9. Tim Etchells, "The Trees: Lovely, Dark, and Deep," *Outside*, November 1999.
10. Oliver, *How to Get It Right*, p. 125.